OXFORD PALAEOGRAPHICAL HANDBOOKS

General Editors

R. W. HUNT   C. H. ROBERTS   F. WORMALD

ENGLISH VERNACULAR HANDS

FROM THE TWELFTH TO THE FIFTEENTH CENTURIES

BY

C. E. WRIGHT

Deputy Keeper, Department of Manuscripts
British Museum

OXFORD
AT THE CLARENDON PRESS

Oxford University Press, Ely House, London W.1

GLASGOW NEW YORK TORONTO MELBOURNE WELLINGTON
CAPE TOWN SALISBURY IBADAN NAIROBI LUSAKA ADDIS ABABA
BOMBAY CALCUTTA MADRAS KARACHI LAHORE DACCA
KUALA LUMPUR SINGAPORE HONG KONG TOKYO

FIRST PUBLISHED 1960

REPRINTED LITHOGRAPHICALLY IN GREAT BRITAIN
AT THE UNIVERSITY PRESS, OXFORD
BY VIVIAN RIDLER
PRINTER TO THE UNIVERSITY
1969

PREFACE

THIS volume is intended to illustrate the development of the English vernacular hands from about 1100 to approximately 1470, that is, a few years before Caxton established his printing-press at Westminster (1477). Wherever possible, dated manuscripts have been selected for reproduction, but the selection has also been conditioned by the desire to put before students specimens from Middle English works with which they will be most familiar textually; hence the choice of the well-known rather than the unfamiliar. Each plate is accompanied by a transcription, preceded by a brief description of the text, such details of the manuscript as are relevant to the present purpose (that is, omitting such data as gatherings, prickings, &c.), and a note calling attention to special features of the handwriting.

The purpose of the introduction, which has been kept to a minimum, is to supply the student, firstly, with a sketch of the background as seen from the point of view of the manuscripts in which the texts of our medieval English literature have been preserved, and, secondly, with a palaeographical section, in the form of a very brief general statement of some of the chief features of the handwriting, the details being easily—and most profitably—studied in the facsimiles themselves and their accompanying notes. It is hoped that in this way the student will see the subject of vernacular handwriting in its proper perspective, as an essential part of the study of Middle English language and literature.

In preparing this volume I am especially grateful to my wife for her constant encouragement and for help in innumerable ways; I am also deeply indebted to Dr. F. E. Harmer, F.B.A., who has read through the typescript of this volume (with the exception of the transcriptions) and has made a number of most valuable suggestions; lastly my thanks are due to the Trustees of the British Museum and the Curators of the Bodleian Library, Oxford, for their courtesy in allowing the reproduction of pages from manuscripts in their possession, and to the staff of the Clarendon Press for the care they have given to the many difficult problems involved in the layout and printing.

C. E. WRIGHT

London,
April 1959

c

CONTENTS

INTRODUCTION

I. THE VERNACULAR MANUSCRIPT TRADITION

ENGLAND is particularly rich in the vernacular manuscripts that have survived from the Middle Ages. This is in spite of losses that must have been going on continuously throughout the period either through wastage due to normal day-by-day use, through neglect, through changes of taste, or through periodical spells of deliberate destruction (for instance, of Wycliffite and Lollard manuscripts in the late fourteenth and early fifteenth centuries). In the post-medieval period the wanton havoc that involved manuscripts of all kinds as an accompaniment of the Reformation must also be remembered. These vernacular manuscripts belong not only to the centuries following the Norman Conquest but to the Anglo-Saxon period as well, so that a manuscript tradition is, in spite of the cataclysm of 1066, continuously present from the ninth century until the *written* literary work was gradually superseded by the *printed* in the latter decades of the fifteenth century; for, wrote Robert Hegge, 'since the art of Printing was invented, whereby men after a more cheap way could attaine to some superficial Learning; old manuscripts were bequeathed to the *Mothes*: and *Pigeons*, and *Jack-dawes* became the only students in Church libraries: and bookes were wounded with pen knifes for their pictures, with as great cruelty as *Cassia*, or *Johannes Scotus* martyred by their own Schollers.'[1]

This manuscript tradition in England for vernacular works is exceptional in its continuity from so early a date, being quite unequalled by the rest of Europe. Iceland, which produced in the Middle Ages the richest vernacular literature among the Germanic peoples, offers the closest parallel to England, from which indeed the Icelandic scribes in their earliest work were strongly influenced. The manuscript tradition there is continuous from the twelfth century, the Copenhagen MS., Arnamagnæan MS. 237, in all probability the oldest of all surviving Icelandic manuscripts, having been written about 1150, while the oldest extant manuscript of any size is the *Homiliu-Bók*, now preserved in the Royal Library at Stockholm (Perg. 4to No. 15), which was written about 1200 or a little earlier. The *Codex Regius* of the Poetic Edda dates from about 1250. In quantity and in earliness of date the Icelandic vernacular is rivalled by the rich literature in Old Irish, for which the earliest manuscript of the great collections of romances, the *Leabhar na h-Uidre* (*Book of the Dun Cow*), was written at Clonmacnois about 1100. Manuscripts for Anglo-Norman literature are continuous from the first half of the twelfth

---

[1] Robert Hegge, *The Legend of St. Cuthbert*, London, 1663, pp. 43, 44.

century, while for the rest it may suffice to note that for French medieval literature the earliest manuscript of perhaps its greatest ornament, the *Chanson de Roland* (which in its present form dates from about 1080), was probably written between 1130 and 1140 (Oxford, Bodleian, Digby 23).

In spite of the Norman Conquest English continued as the spoken language among the lower classes and to a lesser degree elsewhere. On the evidence brought together by R. M. Wilson, it is, I think, impossible to do otherwise than accept his conclusion that 'during the period up to 1300 English probably remained the sole language of the lower classes; many of the middle and upper classes and lower clergy were probably bilingual, speaking English and French, or English and Latin: amongst the higher clergy trilingualism was probably not uncommon', and that 'it seems fairly clear that the displacement of English, as a spoken language, by French is unsupported by any considerable body of evidence'.[1] This realistic conclusion makes it easier to understand, and to see in its proper historical perspective, the continued copying of Old English texts and some versions of the *Chronicle*. Thus the turn of the eleventh century is represented by the manuscript (Brit. Mus., Cotton Tiberius B. iv) of the Worcester version[2] (usually designated E) of the *Anglo-Saxon Chronicle*. Though it comes to an end with the annal for 1079, E was in fact copied about 1100, that is some five years after the death of the last Anglo-Saxon Bishop of Worcester, St. Wulfstan (d. 1095), whose life, be it noted, when it came to be written in 1113 by Colman was composed in *English*. The linguistic transition is more fully illustrated by the Peterborough extension of the *Chronicle* named after that place (Bodleian, Laud Misc. 636) and usually cited as D, which, covering the years 1121–54, was written up by two hands between 1121 and 1155. The basis of its earlier portion was a lost manuscript from St. Augustine's, Canterbury, borrowed by Peterborough after a destructive fire there in 1116.[3] Thus its last annal carries us as far as the end of Stephen's reign and the accession of Henry II. Suggestive of the changes taking place is also the fact that the Canterbury Epitome of the *Chronicle* (designated F) (Brit. Mus., Cotton Domitian A. viii), written about 1100, is bilingual— English and Latin.

Meanwhile, Old English texts were being copied well on through the twelfth century. From early in the century and probably from south-east

---

[1] *History* (N.S.), xxvii (1943), p. 60.

[2] It has recently been argued with great cogency, however, that the origin of this chronicle was York: see D. Whitelock in introduction to the facsimile of the *Peterborough Chronicle* (Early English Manuscripts in Facsimile, iv, 1954), pp. 28–30, and F. E. Harmer's review in *Review of English Studies* (N.S.), viii (1957), pp. 51–54.

[3] On the linguistic strata of the *Peterborough Chronicle* and the Chronicle's significance for the continuing influence of the West-Saxon literary tradition after the Conquest see C. Clark, 'Studies in the Vocabulary of the *Peterborough Chronicle*, 1070–1154', *English and Germanic Studies*, v (1952–3), pp. 67–89, and 'Notes on MS. Laud. Misc. 636', *Medium Ævum*, xxiii (1954), pp. 71–75.

England comes a manuscript of the Alfredian version of Boethius' *De Consolatione Philosophiae* (Bodleian, Bodley 180, *S.C.* 2079), which is now our only authority for the prose version of the Latin *metra* since the loss of the Cotton MS. in the fire of 1731. From the third quarter of the century dates the manuscript of the collection of Old English sermons, chiefly Ælfric's, known as the 'Bodley Homilies' (Bodleian, Bodley 343, *S.C.* 2406 C); and from a slightly later period in the century come the 'Hatton Gospels' (Bodleian, Hatton 38, *S.C.* 4090). The latter were copied from what is now Brit. Mus. Royal I A. xiv, itself a twelfth-century transcript of a manuscript of the Gospels of *c.* 1050 (now Bodleian, Bodley 441, *S.C.* 2382). From well on in the century dates also the material in the first part (Codex I) of the famous *Beowulf* MS. (Brit. Mus., Cotton Vitellius A. xv) and the copy of Ælfric's sermons in Brit. Mus., Cotton Vespasian D. xiv.[1] But that the vernacular in its pre-Conquest form was becoming unfamiliar is to be seen from the fact that the Old English homilies, copied in Bodleian, Hatton 116 (*S.C.* 5136) in the second half of the twelfth century, probably at Worcester, were being furnished with Latin glosses by the famous Worcester 'tremulous hand' in the early thirteenth century.[2]

The strength of the vernacular's position, however, is demonstrated by the fact that from this very time—about 1200—date the manuscripts of some of the most important and famous of our Middle English texts; for instance, the remarkable manuscript (Bodleian, Junius I, *S.C.* 5113) of the East Midland work, *Ormulum* (almost certainly in part autograph), and the manuscript of our earliest Middle English dialogue, *Vices and Virtues*, in Brit. Mus., Stowe 34 (probably a north-east Essex text). Both are followed closely but with less clearly definable limits as to date by the manuscript of the Kentish text, entitled from its manuscript (Brit. Mus., Cotton Vespasian A. xxii) the 'Vespasian Hymns'. Then in quick succession come the chief surviving manuscripts of the texts of the *Ancrene Riwle*: from the first quarter of the thirteenth century that in Brit. Mus., Cotton Titus D. xviii, and from the second quarter

---

[1] See also R. W. Chambers, 'On the Continuity of English Prose', in E.E.T.S. o.s. no. 186, 1932, especially pp. xc ff.

[2] See *Early Worcester MSS.*, ed. C. H. Turner, Oxford, 1916, pp. lvi, lvii; S. J. Crawford, 'The Worcester Marks and Glosses of the O.E. MSS. in the Bodleian', *Anglia*, lii (1928), pp. 1–25; N. R. Ker, 'The Date of the "Tremulous" Worcester Hand', *Leeds Studies in English and Kindred Languages*, no. 6 (1937), pp. 28, 29. The significance of the 'tremulous' Worcester scribe is well summed up by Crawford thus: 'He was a good Latin scholar (the majority of his glosses are in that tongue) acquainted with Anglo-Norman, and, what was becoming rarer, he possessed a competent knowledge of Old English—at any rate of the prose speech. Unfortunately we have no evidence that he was interested in poetry. On his own lines, he deserves to be mentioned with his (probably) slightly younger and more romantic contemporary Laȝamon of Ar(e)ley Regis, as one of those forgotten scholars who made the Worcester district at the close of the 12th century a centre of literary activity and kept alive the tradition of Anglo-Saxon literature, which rendered possible the splendid revival of the 14th century in the west and south-west of England.'

those in Brit. Mus., Cotton Nero A. xiv and Cotton Cleopatra C. vi (to which period belongs also the *Ancrene Wisse* version preserved in Cambridge, Corpus Christi College 402); while from approximately the middle of the same century date the manuscripts of the A text of Laȝamon's *Brut* from the West Midlands (Brit. Mus., Cotton Caligula A. ix, fols. 1–194^v) and of the famous Surrey or Sussex poem of *The Owl and the Nightingale* (preserved in the same manuscript at fols. 233–46).

All these important vernacular manuscripts date almost certainly from before 1258, the year in which Henry III issued in English, as well as in French, his proclamation confirming the Provisions of Oxford. The use of English in this document, which 'marks the momentary emergence of English as an official language',[1] may have been partially due to the nationalist reaction occurring in Henry III's reign, most spectacularly expressed in the politics of Simon de Montfort, though affecting also art and architecture.[2] This reaction was, however, temporary and the use of English as an official language only emerges well on in the fourteenth century in Chaucer's lifetime. In 1362 Edward III decreed that cases should be pleaded in English, because French was too little known, and in 1386 English makes a first appearance in a Petition to Parliament. The Lord Chancellor opened Parliament in English speeches in 1362, 1363, and 1364. Yet it was not until after 1444 that English appears regularly in petitions and only after 1484 were the Statutes recorded in the vernacular. Margaret Deanesley notes[3] that 'the first English sentence in the collection of *London Wills* occurs in a will dated 1405, and directs that a chantry priest should ask for prayers for the founder in English'. The evidence of Trevisa in a significant note in his translation of 1385 of Higden's *Polychronicon*, composed in 1364, shows that children were at that date learning in English in the grammar schools.[4] Inscriptions on monumental brasses document the increasing use and final victory of English: the earliest in verse is that at Brightwell Baldwin, Oxfordshire, to John the Smith and his family, *c.* 1370,[5] and in prose that at Wanlip, Leicestershire, to Sir Thomas Walsch and his wife, 1393.[6] The earliest deed in Middle English dates from 1376 and relates to Ramsbury in Wiltshire (Brit. Mus., Harley Charter 45. A. 37).[7]

---

[1] See *Early Middle English Texts*, ed. B. Dickins and R. M. Wilson, London, 1951, pp. 7–9. For a facsimile see New Palaeographical Society, ser. ii, pl. 73. Two of the English copies survive, one in the Bodleian Library and one in the Public Record Office.

[2] See P. Brieger, *English Art, 1216–1307* (Oxford History of English Art, vol. iv, 1957), *passim.*   [3] *The Lollard Bible*, Cambridge, 1920, p. 205.

[4] Quoted, for instance, by Toller, *History of the English Language*, Cambridge, 1904, p. 212. See R. Higden, *Polychronicon*, Rolls Series, no. 41, vol. ii, pp. 160, 161: 'children of gramer scole conneþ na more Frensche þan can hir lift heele.'

[5] Printed by H. Haines, *A Manual of Monumental Brasses*, i (1861), p. cxli.

[6] See J. Nichols, *The History and Antiquities of . . . Leicestershire*, vol. iii, pt. 2 (1804), pl. cxlvi (opp. p. 1097).   [7] See L. Morsbach, in *An English Miscellany*, Oxford, 1901, pp. 347–54.

These facts are very relevant to a consideration of the production of vernacular manuscripts and make all the more remarkable the number that remain.

It is interesting that to the very date or thereabouts of the *momentary* emergence of English as the official language belongs the manuscript leaf (Brit. Mus., Harley 978, fol. 11ᵛ) on which is written, with its music, one of the most famous of English lyrics, the *Cuckoo Song* beginning 'Sumer is icumen in', the provenance of which is almost certainly Reading in Berkshire and the date *c.* 1260.[1] This poem is a foretaste of the splendid lyric outburst of fifty years later, the 'Harley Lyrics', which are preserved in a manuscript (Brit. Mus., Harley 2253) that may be dated to the decade following the Battle of Bannockburn (1314).[2]

In the fourteenth century we pass to manuscripts that are sometimes not only more precisely datable but may even be specifically dated. In the same way also we are able to put a name to individual authors and occasionally through autographs to come closer to their personality. Thus, from the 1320's comes what is possibly the autograph manuscript of the poems of Friar William Herbert, who died in 1333 (Brit. Mus., Additional 46919)[3] and the manuscript of the Chronicle (longer version) of a Robert (of Gloucester) who 'was wel sore aferd' on the day of the Battle of Evesham (1265) and whose intensity of feeling here and there in his recasting of the Chronicle clothes him with personality even if his habitat be but inferential (Brit. Mus., Cotton Caligula A. xi). And from 1340 (the probable birth-year of Chaucer) comes our first dated and first certainly autograph manuscript (Brit. Mus., Arundel 57), that of the *Ayenbite of Inwyt*, which was written by its author, Michael of Northgate, a monk of St. Augustine's Abbey, Canterbury, in that year.[4] From this period onwards it becomes normal for several manuscripts to be available for a text, and yet the great group of alliterative poems from north-west England, which includes *Sir Gawain and the Green Knight*, is preserved in only one manuscript from the end of this century (Brit. Mus., Cotton Nero A. x). Nevertheless, for the more popular writers and works of the later fourteenth and the fifteenth centuries the number of manuscripts increases tremendously. No less than 170 manuscripts remain of the Wycliffite translations of the Old and New Testaments (notwithstanding in this case the officially

[1] See B. Schofield, 'The Provenance and Date of "Sumer is icumen in" ', *The Music Review*, ix (1948), pp. 81–86.

[2] See G. L. Brooke, *The Harley Lyrics*, Manchester, 1948, especially p. 3. The Battle of Bannockburn is referred to in a version of the 'Prophecies' of Thomas of Erceldoune.

[3] This manuscript was formerly Phillipps MS. 8336. For facsimiles and an account of the manuscript see Catalogue 79 [1950] of W. H. Robinson Ltd. of Pall Mall, London.

[4] This manuscript, with some twenty others, was given by Michael to his monastery (see M. R. James, *The Ancient Libraries of Canterbury and Dover*, Cambridge, 1903, p. lxxvii); the St. Augustine's pressmark is on fol. 4ʳ of the Arundel MS.

sponsored campaign of destruction), and of works by or associated with Rolle we possess large numbers of manuscripts—38 of his *Form of Perfect Living*, 40 of his Commentary on the Psalter, while of the pseudo-Rolle *Pricke of Conscience* (*Stimulus Conscientie*) over 100 are extant. For Langland's *Piers Plowman* at least 60 manuscripts survive, and for Chaucer's *Canterbury Tales* 82 manuscripts are listed by Manly and Rickert.

Besides the disappearance of the anonymity of authors and the presence of autograph manuscripts, we now meet more frequently with the names of scribes. In a late fourteenth-century manuscript of the *Cursor Mundi* in the Bodleian Library (Fairfax 14, *S.C.* 3894) is this colophon (fol. 123ᵛ): 'Stokyn-brig scripsit istum librum Willelmo Keruour de Lanc[astria].' The following better-known examples may also be noted: Robert Thornton, who wrote about 1440 the manuscript of romances, now known by his name, preserved in Lincoln Cathedral Library (MS. A. 1. 17 (A. 5. 2));[1] Thomas Hoccleve, scribe as well as poet (?1370–?1430);[2] John Shirley, an enthusiastic admirer of Chaucer and a professional scribe, who wrote several manuscripts, including, in 1440, Brit. Mus., Additional 5467 (see fol. 97).[3] William Ebesham wrote a number of volumes for Sir John Paston (who died in 1479), including parts of Brit. Mus., Lansdowne 285 (see, for example, fol. 136, 'Quod W. Ebesham'), which can be identified with 'the Great Book' cited among the items for which he claimed payment in a letter written to Sir John Paston in 1469.[4] There is also John Farnelay who wrote in 1405 the manuscript of the *Pricke of Conscience* now preserved in Brit. Mus., Additional 32578 (fols. 1–103).

2. THE HANDWRITING

After the Conquest, at first consistently and then sporadically, the significant characteristics of the Anglo-Saxon hand continued until about 1200. After that the handwriting is materially different in individual features and in general character. In the twelfth-century vernacular manuscripts the three characteristic forms of *f* (ꝼ), *g* (ᵹ), and *r* (ꞃ) continue. In the individualistic

[1] For facsimile see New Pal. Soc., ser. ii, pl. 45, and on Thornton see *D.N.B.* lvi (1898), pp. 303, 304. Thornton was also concerned with Brit. Mus. Additional MS. 31042 (on which see *Cat. of Additions to Manuscripts Dept. of B.M., 1876–1881*, pp. 148–51).

[2] H. C. Schulz, 'Thomas Hoccleve, Scribe', *Speculum*, xii (1937), pp. 71–81.

[3] H. S. Bennett, *Chaucer and the Fifteenth Century* (Oxford History of English Literature, vol. ii, pt. 1, 1947), pp. 116–18, 298.

[4] On Ebesham as scribe see A. I. Doyle, 'The Work of a Late Fifteenth-century English Scribe, William Ebesham', *Bulletin of the John Rylands Library*, xxxix (1957), pp. 298–325. Also H. S. Bennett, *The Pastons and their England*, Cambridge, 1922, pp. 112, 113. The letter is no. 596 in Gairdner's edition of the Paston Letters (see also Everyman's Library edition, 1951 reprint, vol. ii, pp. 38–40, and *Paston Letters*, ed. N. Davis, Oxford, 1958, no. 51).

hand of the *Ormulum* MS. (see no. 2) they are almost aggressively present, but it should be noted that the second hand of the *Peterborough Chronicle* (see no. 1), writing probably in 1155, does not use them. Naturally the two Anglo-Saxon runic letters 'wyn' (ᵽ = *w*) and 'thorn' (þ = *th*), and the crossed or barred *d* (Đ, ð = *th*) persist. Of the two the ᵽ became increasingly infrequent in the thirteenth century and disappeared entirely about 1300, making a few very rare appearances in the Havelok MS. (Bodleian, Laud Misc. 108).[1] Its place was taken by *w* (double *v*). The þ survived until the fifteenth century in two forms. First it was in a mutilated version, caused by the loss of the upper portion of the vertical stroke or ascender. This gave it a shape indistinguishable from ᵽ (wyn). Then as early as 1300–25 it is found in a *y* form, the *y* proper being sometimes dotted (*ẏ*) in order to prevent misinterpretation. The appearance in modern times of 'ye' as a pseudo-archaism for 'the' is derived from this. Crossed *d* (ð) survived until about the end of the thirteenth century. It should be observed that þ and ᵽ are a frequent source of scribal error and of mistakes in transcription owing to the careless writing of þ, the upper portion of the vertical being often omitted from the thirteenth century onwards (see e.g. no. 10). The insular *g* (ᵹ) continued beside the continental *g*, but in the modified form ȝ (with the name 'yok' or 'yogh': see notes to no. 17)[2] was employed medially or finally for a number of sounds—for example, for the *gh* (back spirant) sound as in 'kniȝt' or medially after *a* or *o* for the *w* sound or initially for the *y*-sound (initial front spirant), as in 'ȝeo', 'ȝer'. Under this guise the letter persisted into the fifteenth century; occasionally ȝ was utilized for *s* or *z* (see e.g. nos. 9, 10, 15, 17). The insular *r*-form (ɼ) disappeared very early and was replaced by two kinds: a 2-form (ɞ) and the continental form (r). The former is most common in final positions, particularly after *o* (which suggests a relationship with the abbreviation ꝛ for *-rum* in Latin texts), and develops from about 1400 onwards a more elaborate form with a hook below the line (thus ꝫ). The characteristic insular *s* of the Anglo-Saxon hand (ſ) is not exemplified in the facsimile (see no. 1) from the *Peterborough Chronicle* MS.; it had been used by the first scribe but disappeared entirely in the second scribe's work. The long *s* of the Anglo-Saxon hand (sometimes very exaggerated in form) persists, however, with some modification of its extravagance and towards the end of the period lost the little tag to the left. The modern form (*s*) appears by 1100 (e.g. in the *Textus Roffensis*) and in our examples is

[1] See *The Lay of Havelok the Dane*, ed. W. W. Skeat and K. Sisam, Oxford, 2nd ed., 1923, p. ix.

[2] On this letter see A. C. Paues, 'The Name of the Letter ȝ', *Modern Language Review*, vi (1911), pp. 441–54, and *O.E.D.* under G, Y(2), and Yogh, and for the precise philological sounds for which it was used in Middle English see (*inter alia*) J. and E. M. Wright, *An Elementary Middle English Grammar*, 1923, pp. 13, 14; G. L. Brook, *Notes on Some English Sound-changes*, 1945 reprint, p. 15, but especially E. V. Gordon's edition of *Pearl*, Oxford, 1953, pp. 91–93.

already present in the *Ormulum* MS. (of *c.* 1200) (see no. 2). It is used normally in final position for the greater part of the period. Later there appears a third form, the Greek *s* (σ), at first finally (see no. 9). This derives from the court-hand, whose influence is at work on the vernacular book-hands throughout almost the whole of the Middle English period, some of the literary texts being actually written in it, e.g. the 'Harley Lyrics' (see no. 9). In writing the vernacular the English scribes were influenced by the two main types of hand used for writing in Latin: the book-hand and the more current business hands. In the specimens written before 1300 it will be seen that book-hand pre-dominates, though no. 3 is closely related to contemporary cursive writing. In the fourteenth century there can be seen clearer influence of cursive combined with a tendency to produce a combination of the two elements. Thus a hand may be nearer to cursive in individual letter forms, but at the same time its regularity and the fact that the letters are more formal brings it closer to book-hand. By the fifteenth century a definitely vernacular book-hand has appeared which can show every gradation of form from cursive to formal Gothic script.

As regards the dating of vernacular MSS. it must be stated frankly and by way of warning that (where no internal evidence is available) this is to be regarded for the most part as tentative only; on this subject I cannot do better than quote here for emphasis a statement recently made by one of our greatest living palaeographers.

'In palaeography', writes Dr. Lowe, 'we mostly splash about in a sea of uncertainty or complete nescience: our ignorance is such that we cling to straws. Every now and then, however, we sight a raft which by careful steering takes us to *terra firma*. Such rafts have been the mainstay of our discipline. They are, of course, our dated and placed manuscripts.'[1]

In the matter of vernacular MSS. we are indeed fortunate in having a number of dated MSS. and for some the provenance or place is known or can be deduced (e.g. Harley 2253), while the dialectal features of their texts suggest frequently and with some reasonable certainty a geographical area of circulation for the MSS. in which the texts occur (e.g. Cotton Nero A. x).

Dates for palaeographical changes in letter forms are never easily come by, especially in book-hands, but by analogy with dated documents it may be ob-served that as regards *t* the vertical stroke which in the twelfth and early thirteenth centuries is always cut short at the cross-bar (τ) seems about 1250–1300 to begin to push above it (t) (see no. 10), and this development helps in distinguishing *c* and *t*, between which confusion is not uncommon; again, we may notice that the upper bow of *a* (λ) tends to bend down on the lower bowl and so by a little after 1250 the letter is closed (see no. 7) and we have next

[1] E. A. Lowe, 'A Key to Bede's Scriptorium', *Scriptorium*, xii (1958), p. 182.

a completely enclosed letter like an angular figure 8 (see no. 11). This last is seen in its most exaggerated form in the liturgical hands.

Minim letters either singly or in combination (*n* and *u*, *nu* and *un*, &c.) are frequently difficult to distinguish and the possibility of confusion is increased by the absence from *i* of that dot to which we are today accustomed. In order to obviate on the reader's part the misinterpretation likely to occur therefore in such combinations as *m* and *in*, &c. the scribe early developed the practice of introducing as a diacritic mark over the *ı* a slanting stroke like an acute accent (*í*), a practice taken over even by the early printers (e.g. Caxton), the later printers however reducing it to the round dot with which we are now familiar. In order to emphasize this feature the medieval scribal practice is followed precisely throughout this book in the printing of the transcriptions: that is to say, undotted *i* (*ı*) or accented *i* (*í*) is printed as and when used by the scribe.

Abbreviations, contractions, or suspensions in vernacular MSS. are few in number. In the transcriptions in this volume it was thought preferable to leave them unexpanded, but they are of course interpreted and commented on as necessary in the palaeographical notes at the head of each transcription. A brief general statement on them may, however, be not out of place here. The majority of them have been taken over from practices used in Latin MSS. In the specimens given here it will be seen that a line over a letter usually indicates the omission of 'm' or 'n', and that 'er', 're', or 'ur' omitted are shown by a loop written above the line. p = per, ꝑ = pro, ꝓ = pre are also quite frequently found. There are some which occasionally offer difficulties. Some are simple, as þ or þᵗ for *þæt*, þᵘ for *þou*, wᵗ for *with*, sometimes þoñ for *þone*. The letter *r* which occurs so frequently is often omitted and its nearest vowel written above the line, hence *a*-suprascript means *ra* and the symbol ꝏ (as used in Latin MSS.) above a consonant or vowel signifies *ur*. These and other abbreviations are illustrated abundantly in the facsimiles. Final symbols also offer trouble: for example, a final curl (ę) signifies -*es* in southern English manuscripts and -*is* or -*ys* in northern; a final ꝯ signifies -*us*; and under this heading comes the ever difficult problem of the final -*e* that is sometimes indicated by a tag or tail attached to the preceding consonant (which, however, in some cases is entirely meaningless) and sometimes by a horizontal stroke through the upper verticals of letters like *l*—for example, aƚƚ = *alle*.

Space does not allow for a discussion of the palaeographical terms used here and in the notes (such as court-hand, Tironian nota, &c.) but an explanation of these is readily available in the books referred to in the Select Bibliography (p. xix), especially in those marked with an asterisk.

Under the entry 'Text' in the Notes to the plates the practice has been, for the sake of brevity and to avoid a multiplicity of references, to cite the standard edition(s) of the *complete* text, but the student should observe that nearly all the passages quoted, or ones similar, are to be found in one or other or all of the following volumes of selections:

O. F. EMERSON, *A Middle English Reader*, London, 1905, &c.

J. HALL, *Selections from Early Middle English*, *1130–1250*, Oxford, 1920, &c.

K. SISAM, *Fourteenth Century Prose and Verse* (with glossary by J. R. R. TOLKIEN), Oxford, 1925, &c.

B. DICKINS and R. M. WILSON, *Early Middle English Texts*, London, 1951, &c.

SELECT BIBLIOGRAPHY

Note. Palaeographical works (or articles) which include no account of the vernacular as distinct from the Latin hands are deliberately omitted from the following selective list (hence the omission, for example, of E. A. Lowe's contribution on handwriting to *The Legacy of the Middle Ages*, 1926). The works which discuss palaeographical terms in detail are marked with an asterisk.

T. ASTLE, *The Origin and Progress of Writing* (London, 1784; repr. 1803, 1820).

The Palaeographical Society. *Facsimiles of Manuscripts and Inscriptions*, ed. E. A. BOND, E. M. THOMPSON, and G. F. WARNER (London). 1st series, 1873–83; 2nd series, 1884–94; Indexes, 1901.

W. W. SKEAT, *Twelve Facsimiles of Old English Manuscripts* (Oxford, 1892).

E. M. THOMPSON, 'The History of English Handwriting, A.D. 700–1400', *Trans. of the Bibliographical Society*, v (1898–1900), pp. 110–42, 213–53.

F. G. KENYON, *Facsimiles of Biblical Manuscripts in the British Museum* (London, 1900).

The New Palaeographical Society. *Facsimiles of Ancient Manuscripts*, &c., ed. E. M. THOMPSON, G. F. WARNER, and J. P. GILSON (London). 1st series, 1903–12; 2nd series, 1913–32; Indexes, 1914, 1932.

*E. M. THOMPSON, *Handbook of Greek and Latin Palaeography* (London, 3rd ed., 1906).

A. C. PAUES, 'Runes and Manuscripts', *The Cambridge History of English Literature* (Cambridge), vol. i (1907), chap. ii.

*E. M. THOMPSON, *An Introduction to Greek and Latin Palaeography* (Oxford, 1912).

*C. JOHNSON and H. JENKINSON, *English Court Hand A.D. 1066–1500* (Oxford, 1915).

FALCONER MADAN, 'Handwriting', *Mediaeval England*, ed. H. W. C. Davis (Oxford, 1924), pp. 451–69.

H. JENKINSON, *The Later Court Hands in England from the 15th to the 17th Century* (Cambridge, 1927).

J. M. MANLY and E. RICKERT, *The Text of the Canterbury Tales* (Michigan, 1940), vol. i.

*N. DENHOLM-YOUNG, *Handwriting in England and Wales* (Cardiff, 1954).

LIST OF PLATES AND TRANSCRIPTIONS

hæued. 7 uuryþen it ðat it gæde to þe hærnes. Hi diden heom in quar-
terne þar nadres 7 snakes 7 pades wæron inne, 7 drapen heom swa.
Sume hi diden in crucethus, ðat is in an cæste þat was scort 7 nareu
7 undep, 7 dide scærpe stanes þerinne, 7 þrengde þe man þerinne. ðat him bræcon alle þe limes. In mani of þe castles wæron lof
7 grin, ðat wæron rachenteges ðat twa oþer thre men hadden onoh to
bæron onne. þat was swa maced ðat is fæstned to an beom, 7 diden an
scærp iren abuton þa mannes throte 7 his hals, ðat he ne myhte nowi-
derwardes, ne sitten ne lien ne slepen, oc bæron al ðat iren. Mani
þusen hi drapen mid hunger. I ne can ne i ne mai tellen alle þe
wunder ne alle þe pines ðat hi diden wrecce men on þis land, 7 ðat laste-
de þa .xix. wintre wile Stephne was king, 7 æure it was uuerse 7
uuerse. Hi læiden gæildes o the tunes æure umwile 7 clepeden it
tenserie. þa þe wrecce men ne hadden nämore to gyuen, þa ræueden hi 7 brendon alle the tunes, ðat wel þu myhtes faren al a dæis
fare, sculdest thu neure finden man in tune sittende, ne land ti-
led. þa was corn dære, 7 flec 7 cæse 7 butere, for nan ne wæs o þe land.
Wrecce men sturuen of hunger, sume ieden on ælmes þe waren sum
wile ricemen, sume flugen ut of lande. Wes næure gæt mare wrec-
ched on land, ne næure hethen men werse ne diden þan hi diden.
for ouer sithon ne for baren hi nouther cyrce ne cyrceiærd, oc namen
al þe god ðat þarinne was, 7 brenden sythen þe cyrce 7 altegædere.
Ne hi ne forbaren b[iscopes] land ne abb[otes] ne preostes, ac ræueden munekes
7 clerekes, 7 æuric man other þe ouermyhte. Gif twa men oþer .iii.
coman ridend to an tun, al þe tunscipe flugen for heom. wenden ð[at]
hi wæron ræueres. þe biscopes 7 lered men heom cursede æure, oc was
heom naht þar of, for hi uueron al for cursæd 7 forsuoren 7 forlo-
ren. War sæ me tilede, þe erthe ne bar nan corn, for þe land was al
fordon mid suilce dædes, 7 hi sæden openlice ðat Crist slep, 7 his ha-
lechen. Suilc 7 mare þanne we cunnen sæin, we þolenden .xix. wintre
                                                    7 for ure sinnes.

1. Oxford, Bodleian Library, Laud MS. Misc. 636

PETERBOROUGH VERSION of the ANGLO-SAXON CHRONICLE (MS. E): written at various dates by two scribes between A.D. 1121 and A.D. 1155 at Peterborough, based as to its earlier portion on a MS. borrowed from St. Augustine's Abbey, Canterbury.

Written shortly after the accession of Henry II, probably in A.D. 1155, by the *second* scribe who added the annals A.D. 1132–A.D. 1154 (fols. 88ᵛ–91ᵛ).

Vellum: 21 × 14 cm.

A heavy, compressed book-hand, strongly twelfth-century in character but rather lifeless.

Note. In contrast to the *first* scribe the present one does *not* use the insular forms of *a* (ᴧ), *f* (ŗ), *g* (ᵹ), and *r* (ŗ) but their Caroline forms. For *d* he uses both Caroline (d) and insular form (ð); after *o* he uses regularly the 2-form of *r*; his *s* has various forms of Caroline *s* besides the round *s* in final position; þ and ð are used but *th* is much more common than in the hand of the first scribe; 'wyn' (þ) is common but so also is *uu*; æ is normal but some examples of ę occur.

Abbreviations: for *and* he uses the Tironian nota 7 with a curved head and for *þæt* he uses ð.

Text printed in: *Two of the Saxon Chronicles Parallel*, ed. J. Earle and C. Plummer (Oxford, 1892), i, pp. 3–269 *passim*.

Complete facsimile in: *The Peterborough Chronicle*, ed. D. Whitelock (Early English Manuscripts in Facsimile, vol. iv, Copenhagen, 1954).

Our plate shows fol. 89ᵛ (the Anglo-Norman text written in the margins is omitted) (text, part of the entry under A.D. 1137).

TRANSCRIPTION

hæued . 7 uurýþen it ð it gæde to þe ʰærnes . Hi diden heð inquar-
terne þar nadres 7 snakes 7 pades pæron inne . 7 drapen heð spa .
Sume hi diden in crucethus ð is in an cęste þat pas scort 7 nareu .
7 undep . 7 dide scærpe stanes þerinne . 7 þrengde þe man þær
inne . ð hī bræcon alle þe limes . In mani of þe castles pæron lof
7 grī . ð pæron rachenteges ð tpa oþer thre men hadden onoh to
bæron onne . þat pas sua maced . ð is fæstned to an beom . 7 diden an
scærp iren abuton þa mannes throte 7 his hals . ð he ⁿᵉ mýhte nopi-
derpardes . ne sitten ne lien ne slepen . oc bæron al ð iren . Mani
þusen hi drapen mid hungær . I ne can ne í ne mai tellen alle þe
punder ne alle þe pines ð hi diden preccemen on þis land . 7 ð laste-
de þa . xix . þintre þile Stephne pas king 7 æure it pas uuerse 7
uuerse . Hi læiden gæildes oⁿ the tunes æure upile 7 clepeden it
tenserie . Þa þe uureccemen ne hadden nã more to gýuen . þa ræueden hi 7 brendon alle the tunes . ð pel þu mýhtes faren al a dæis
fare sculdest thu neure finden man in tune sittende . ne land ti-
led . þa pas corn dære . 7 flec 7 cæse 7 butere . for nan ne pæs o þe land .
Þreccemen sturuen of hungær . sume ieden on ælmes þe paren sū
þile ricemen . sume flugen ut of lande . Þes næure gæt mare preĉe
hed on land . ne næure hethen men perse ne diden þan hi diden .
for ouer sithon ne for baren hi nouther circe ne ne cýrceiærd . oc nã
al þe god ð þarinne pas . 7 brenden sýthen þe cýrce 7 altegædere .
Ne hi ne forbaren ƀ land ne abb ne preostes . ac ræueden munekes
7 clerekes . 7 æuric man other þe ouermýhte . Gif tpa men oþer . iii .
coman ridend to an tun . al þe tunscipe flugæn for heð . penden ð
hi pæron ræueres . Þe biscopes 7 leredmen heð cursede æure . oc pas
heð naht þar of . for hi uueron al forcursæd 7 forsuoren 7 forlo-
ren . Þar sæ me tilede . þe erthe ne bar nan corn . for þe land pas al
fordon . mid suilce dædes . 7 hi sæden openlice ð χþist slep . 7 his ha-
lechen . Suilc 7 mare þanne pe cunnen sæin . pe þolenden . xix . þintre
for ure sinnes .

2. Oxford, Bodleian Library, Junius MS. 1

'ORMULUM', a series (imperfect) of homilies on Gospel Lessons, in verse, composed by Orm, an Augustinian Canon, in North-east Midland dialect.

Written probably very early in the thirteenth century.

Vellum: 33/50 × 10/20·3 cm. (a rough vellum, of very varying sizes).

The MS. was written by Orm himself (very probably fols. 3^r–9^r) or under his supervision on the lines of a remarkable orthographical system.

The hand is large, rather heavy, very individualistic and compressed, in direct line of descent from the Anglo-Saxon hand. (The peculiarities of the script are discussed at length by J. E. Turville-Petre, 'Studies in the Ormulum MS.', *Journal of English and Germanic Philology*, vol. xlvi (1947), pp. 1–27.)

Note. Orm uses insular *a* (ᴀ); yogh (ȝ) for *y*-sound, &c.; for hard *g* he uses a form in which the bow under the head is converted into a loop by connecting it to the horizontal stroke (ᵹ); insular *r* (ꞃ), except for overwritten *r* when he uses the continental or Caroline type (e.g. 'broþeꞃ'). He has abandoned insular *f* (ꝼ) for continental *f* (f); long *s* is normal; he uses þ and ꝥ, differentiating them carefully.

Abbreviation very rare, but ꝥ is for *þæt*, and Tironian nota (7) is used for *and*.

Text printed in: *The Ormulum*, with notes and glossary of R. M. White, ed. R. Holt (Oxford, 1878).

Other specimens in: Pal. Soc., ser. ii, pl. 133; W. W. Skeat, *Twelve Facsimiles of Old English Manuscripts* (Oxford, 1892), pl. IV.

Our plate shows fol. 3^r (text, Dedication, lines 1–84).

TRANSCRIPTION

Nu broþerr þallt' . broþeꝛ̄ min .
Afft' þe flæshess kīde . 7 broþeꝛ̄
min ı crısstenndom . þurrh ful-
luhht . 7 þurrh troꝑpe . 7 broþerr min ı godess hus . ȝet o þe þri-
de þise . Þurrh þatt pitt hafenn
tăkeñ ba . an reȝell boc to follȝeñ . Vnn-
derr kanunnkess had . 7 lif . Spa suṁ sannt
appstın sette . Icc̄ hafe don spa suṁ þu badd: 7
forþedd te þı̄ þılle . ¶ Icc̄ hafe peñd ıntıll ennglıssh . Goddspelless hallȝe lare: Afft' þ litle
pitt þatt me . Mın drıhhtın hafeꝑ lenedd .
¶ Þu þohhtesst tatt itt mıhhte þel . Tıll mı-
kell frame turneñ . Ȝiff ennglıssh follc
forr lufe off crist . Itt pollde ȝerne lernenn .
7 follȝeñ itt 7 fillenn itt . Piꝑ þohht piꝑ þord
piꝑ dede . 7 forþi ȝerrndesst tu þ ıcc . þiss þerc̄
þē shollde pırkeñ . 7 ıcc itt hafe forþedd te:
Acc all þurrh crıstess hellpe . 7 uñc bıꝛþ baþe
pañkenn crıst: þ ıtt ıss brohht tıll ende .
¶ Icc hafe saṁnedd o þıss boc . Þa goddspelless neh
alle: þatt sınndenn o þe messeboc . Iñ all þe ȝer
att messe . ¶ 7 aȝȝ affteꝛ̄ þe goddspell stannt . þ
tatt te goddspell meneꝑ . Þatt mann bıꝛꝑ spel-
lenn to þe follc off þeȝȝre saꝑle nede . 7 ȝeꞇ tær tekenn mare ınoh . þu shallt tæronne findenn .
Off þatt tatt crıstess hallȝe þed: Bıꝛꝑ troppeñ
þel . 7 follȝenn . ¶ Icc hafe sett her o þıss boc . amāg
goddspelless þordess . All þurrh me sellfeñ manıȝ
þord . Þerınne spa to fillenn . Acc þu shallt findenn
þatt mın þord . Eȝȝphær þær itt ıss ekedd: Maȝȝ
hellþeñ þa þ redenn itt . To sen . 7 tunndeꝛ̄stanndeñ.

Nu broþerr wallterr. broþerr min.
affterr þe flæshess kinde. Annd broþerr
min i crisstenndom. þurrh ful
luhht annd þurrh trowwþe. Annd bro
þerr min i godess hus. ʒet o þe þri
de wise. þurrh þatt witt hafenn
takenn ba. an reʒhell boc to follʒhenn. Unn
denn kanunnkess had. annd lif. Swa summ sannt
awwstin sette. annd forr þedd te þin wille.
Icc hafe don swa summ þu badd. annd
forrþedd te þin wille. Icc hafe wennd inntill enn
glissh. goddspelless hallʒhe lare. Affterr þatt little
witt tatt me. min drihhtin hafeþþ lenedd.
ʒiff þu þohht tesst tatt itt mihhte wel. till mi
kell frame turnenn. Tiff ennglishh follc
forrlufe off itt. itt wollde ʒerne lernenn.
annd follʒhenn itt. annd fillenn itt. wiþþ þohht wiþþ word
wiþþ dede. Annd forr þi ʒerrndesst tu þiss icc. þiss werrc
þe sholld e wirrkenn. Annd icc itt hafe forrþedd te.
acc all þurrh cristess helpe. annd unnc birrþ baþe
þannkenn crist. þatt itt iss broht till ende.
Icc hafe sammnedd o þiss boc. þa goddspelless neh
alle. þatt sinndenn o þe messe boc. Inn all þe ʒer
att messe. annd aʒʒ affterr þe goddspell stanndeþþ. þatt
tatt te goddspell meneþþ. þatt mann birrþ spel
lenn to þe follc. off þeʒʒre sawle nede. annd ʒet tær
tekenn mare inoh. þu shallt tær onne findenn.
off þatt tatt cristess hallʒhe þed. birrþ trowwenn
wel annd follʒhenn. Icc hafe setted her o þiss boc. amang
goddspelless wordess. All þurrh me sellfenn manig
word. þe rime swa to fillenn. Acc þu shallt findenn
þatt min word. eʒʒ whær þær itt iss ekedd. maʒʒ
hellpenn þa þatt redenn itt. to sen annd tunnderstanndenn.

þanne art tu rihtwis · 7 haue þine godes draednesse mid þe · þ du
þis ne foeliest · þane scule godes ei3e bie uppe þe · þat naðing
ne mai þe derien · 7 his eare opene to þine beues · þat
naþi3 he þe ne pike þar·inen · þus þe rætt þe hali gast þe
spekð · 3iet alþe dai durh þeue selm þe þu 3esikst oðer
iherst bie þar · 3if du þile se þe nele þese hali lare of
þe hali gast underfaden: hlest hwat he seið þar after:

Vt ultius dicit dns sup facietes mala ut disþdat sctam me·
moriam eorz. God þe seið loked yraðliche uppe · he þe euele
doð · þe for his draednesse ne pilleð isþike · for di scal godes
yradðe cume on he · þt hie · hu dit · yrie · And forlesen
hem baðe lif · 7 saule · Of þese deadliche lande þe hie on
puried 7 spa michel luurted · spa hie sculen iet forliese
þat liuiende land · þ is þat eche lif · for dan þe hie nolde
godes lare · hlestene · folзin · Iiet he seið þat here зemiend
scal spo bie forlore · þat me of he ne scal neiðer ne spe·
ken ne þenche · Iiet seið þat hali yrtt · Os timer dns fa·
ci et bona · q aute duri cordis ÷ corruet i malu · Se þe ondrat
god he lat aure þe euel to done for his hette · Se þe is
of hard hierte he nodratt noht god · 7 for di he farð fro
euele to euele · 7 fra senne to senne · hit bieð mani3e me
syiðe besþikene · þat mor draded ane deadliche ma·
ne þane he doð godalmihti · þe for dare yorldes scame
oðer for here scorte liue he alforзeried · 7 slead here du3e
ne saule 7 forliesed þat eche lif · fordi us yarned ihu cst
7 þus seið · Holite time eos q corpus occidit · Anima aute

ne pideidden

ü disþdat de eina
зeinæið e
027.

3. London, British Museum, Stowe MS. 34

'VICES AND VIRTUES', the earliest of all Middle English dialogues, composed in the Essex dialect, about A.D. 1200.

Written about A.D. 1200.

Vellum: 22 × 16 cm.

A vigorous, individualistic hand closely related to the court-hand of the time.

Note. The vertical stroke of the *a* is normally now brought well up but some examples preserve hint of the insular *a* (ᴀ); a remarkable form of *æ* is used, the *e* being suprascript and linked to the top part of the vertical of the *a*; long *s* appears throughout; continental *f* and *r* are now normal; after *o* the 2-form of *r* is used; 'yogh' (ʒ) still preserves in its angularity traces of its origin in the insular *g* (ᵹ); hard *g* is represented by what is now to be the normal form; the insular or uncial *d* (ð) is used; þ and ð are used; þ and ƿ are clearly differentiated; *c* and *t* are well differentiated, the cross-bar of the latter being firmly made (and the vertical does not yet appear above it); *i* has sometimes an upward slanting stroke.

Abbreviations are rare: ꝥ is used for *þæt* and the Tironian nota for *and* is used (7) (in a rather elaborate form ⁊); the horizontal mark of contraction is sometimes hooked at the end.

Correction is by a dot under the letter to be deleted (e.g. *f* in l. 12); this is normal medieval practice.

Text printed in: *Vices and Virtues*, ed. F. Holthausen (E.E.T.S., o.s., nos. 89, 159 (1888, 1921)).

Another specimen in: Pal. Soc., ser. ii, pl. 94.

Our plate shows fol. 20^{r}.

TRANSCRIPTION

ðanne art tu rıhtƿıs ⁊ haue æure godes drædnesse mıd ƿe . ꝥ ðu
ðıs ne forlıes Ðāne sculē godes eıʒē bıē uppe ðe ðat nāðíng
ne maı ðe derıʒē . ⁊ hıs earē opene to ðıne b^{i}enes . ðat
naþīg he ðe ne ƿıle ƿærnen Ðus ðe ratt ðe halıe gast ðe
spekð ʒıet alche daı ðurh ðene selm ðe ðu ʒesıkst oðer-
ıherst bıe ƿar ʒıf ðu ƿıle Se ðe nele ðese halı lare of
ðe halı gast understādeñ ∴ hlest hƿat he seıð ðar after ∴ ne ƿıðealden
Vultus autē dn̄ı suꝑ facıētes mala ut disꝑdat d^{e} tr̄a me-
morıā eoꝝ . Godd he seıð lokeð ƿraðlíche uppe hē ðe euele doð . ðe for hıs dradnesse ne ƿılleð ısƿıkē for ðı scal godes
ƿraððe cumē on hē . ær híe hıt aut ƿıtē and forlıesen
hem baðe lıf^{came} ⁊ saule . Of ðese deadlıche lande ðe hıe on
ƿuníeð ⁊ sƿa mıchel luuíʒeð ∴ sƿa hıe sculen ıec forlíesē
ðat lıuıende land . ꝥ ıs ðat eche lıf . for ðan ðe hıe noldē
godes lare hlestē ne ^{7} folʒın . Gıet he seıð ðat here ʒemíend
scal sƿo hıē forlorē ðat me of hē ne scal neıðer ne sƿe-
ken ne þenchē . Gıet seıð ðat halı ƿrít . *Q^{i} tımet dm̄ facı-*
ū disꝑdat de t'ra *et bona . q̇ autē durı cordıs ÷ corruet ī malū* . Se ðe ondrat
memoriā e godd he lat æure ðe euel to done for hıs heıʒe . Se ðe ıs
oꝝ . of hard^{e} hıerte he nōdratt noht godd . ⁊ for ðı he farð frō
euele to euele . ⁊ frā senne to sēne . hıt bıeð manıʒe mē
sƿıðe besƿıkene ðat more dradeð ane deadlıche mā-
ne ðane he doð god almıhtī . ðe for ðare ƿorldes scame
oðer for here scorte líue hē alforsƿerıeð . ⁊ sleað here auʒe-
ne saule ⁊ forlıeseð ðat eche lıf . forðı us ƿarneð ıħu ċst
⁊ ðus seıð ∴ *Nolıte tım'e eos q̇ corpꝰ occıdūt . anımā autē*

4. London, British Museum, Egerton MS. 613

'POEMA MORALE' (at fols. 64ʳ–70ᵛ), the earlier and shorter form in 370 lines, composed in southern dialect perhaps as early as about A.D. 1150.

Written about A.D. 1225.

Vellum: 22 × 14 cm.

Carefully written rather heavy book-hand.

Note. ʒ and *g* used, former written entirely on the line (compare in this respect and for general similarity of hand those in Cotton MSS. Nero A. xiv and Titus D. xviii ('Ancrene Riwle' MSS.; for latter see plate 5); þ and ƿ (sharply differentiated) and ð used; long *s* only; 2-form of *r* used after *o*; *y* is dotted; in *t* the ascender does not go above the cross-bar; note frequent fusion of *be, de, do* (see note on plate 6); a sort of hook or spur to left of top of the ascenders in *l, h, þ,* &c.) is development of split tops familiar in late twelfth-century hands (cf. Bestiary MS., plate 8).

Abbreviations are rare; note ꝥ for *þæt*. Tironian nota for *and* is in form ⁊.

Text printed in: *Das Frühmittelenglische 'Poema Morale'*, ed. H. Marcus (Palaestra, no. 194, Leipzig, 1934).

Our plate shows fol. 65ᵛ (text, lines 71–97).

TRANSCRIPTION

    god
and óft⟋kan mare þanc ðan ðe hím ʒíuet lesse
  eal hís peorkes ⁊ hís peies ís milce ⁊ rihtpisnesse
líte lác is gode leof . ðe cumeð of gode ipille — *accent*
  ⁊ eðlece muchel ʒíue ðenne ðe heorte is ille — *spacing?*
heuene ⁊ eorðe he oue[r] sihð . his éʒen beoð spo brihte
  Sunne . mone . dei . ⁊ fur . bið þustre to ʒeanes his líhte
nis hī naht for hole . ni húd . spa michel bið his mihte
        n
  nis hit na spá dur⟋e idón . né aspa þustre nihte — *mark misplaced*
    hpet
hé pát⟋deð . ⁊ ðenchet . ealle quike pihte — *mark displaced*
  nis n̄a hlauord spilc se ís crist . na king spílch ure drihte
heouene ⁊ eorðe . ⁊ eal þet is . biloken in his hande
  he deð eal ꝥ his pille ís . á pétere and á lande — *spacing?*
he makede fisces in ðe sé . ⁊ fuʒeles in ðe lufte
  he pít ⁊ pealdeð ealle ðing . ⁊ hé scop ealle ʒesceafte — *spacing!*
he is ord abuten orde . ⁊ ende abuten ende
  hé ane is ǽure enelche stede . pende þer þu pende — *accent*
he is buuen us ⁊ bi neoðen . bi foren ⁊ bi hinde
  þe ðe godes pille deð . eiðer he mei hím finde
elche rune hé ihurð . ⁊ he pat ealle dede
  he ðurh sihð ealches mannes ðanc . phet sceal us to rede
þeðe brekeð godes hése . ⁊ gultet spa ilome
  hpet scule pé seggen oðer don . æt ðe muchele dome
þa ða luueden unriht . ⁊ uuel líf ledde — *spacing*
  hpet scule hí segge oðer dón . ðer engles beoð of dredde
hpet scule pé béren bi foren . mid hpan scule þe cpeman
  pé þe næure gód ne duden . þe heuenliche démen
þer scule beon deofles spa uéle . ðe pulleð us for preʒen

And oft kan mare þanc. þan þe him ȝiuet lesse

eal his weorkes. ⁊ his þeies is milce ⁊ rihtwisnesse

þte lac is gode leof. þe cumeð of gode wille

⁊ eðlete muchel ȝiue þenne þe heorte is ille

euene ⁊ eorðe he oue∙sihð. his eȝen beoð swo brihte

ȝunne. mone. dei. ⁊ fur. bið þustre to ȝæmes his lihte

is hi naht forhole. wi hud. swa muchel bið his mihte

nis hit na swa durne idon. ne aswa þustre mihte

hé þat ȝeð. ⁊ ȝenchet. ealle quike wihte

nis na hlauord swilc se is crist. na king swilch ure drihte

eouene ⁊ eorðe. ⁊ eal þet is. biloken in his hande

he deð eal þ his wille is. a perere and a lande

e makede fisces in þe se. ⁊ fuȝeles in þe lufte

he wit ⁊ wealdeð ealle þing. ⁊ hé scop ealle ȝe sceafte

e is ord abuten orde. ⁊ ende abuten ende

hé ane is æure enelche stede. wende þer þu wende

e is buuen us ⁊ bi neoðen. bi foren ⁊ bi hinde

þe þe godes wille deð. eiðer he mei him finde

lche rune héihurȝ. ⁊ he þat ealle dede

he ðurh sihð ealches mannes ðanc. þwet sceal us to rede

eðe brekeð godes hése. ⁊ gultet swa ilome

hwet scule þe seggen oðer don. æt þe muchele dome

a ða luueden un riht. ⁊ uuel lif ledde

hwet scule hi segge oðer don. ðer engles beoð of dreده

þet scule þe beren bi foren. mid hwan scule þe cweman

þe þe nœure god ne duden. þe heuenliche deinen

er scule beon deofles swa uele. ðe þulleð us for wreȝen

þi mon seruist spareþe uuel. God
hit wile for þi· þ̄ ho beo eadi ead
mod· ⁊ mild haldinge of hi
re selue falle dun to þe eorðe le
ste ho pruide. Þ ȝe hurten
leue childre to þe feorðe dale.
þis eide schulde beo of feole son
diges· for þer beo uttre ⁊ inre· ⁊
eiðer moni falde. Salues þi hw
to wrechen to ȝemes þa· ⁊ bo
te. And hu ȝe as hauel ham
mei gederen of þis dale con
fort ⁊ froure to ȝaines ham
alle. Þat ich þurh þe lare of
þe hali gast mote halde foreȝ
ard· he hit ȝeat me þurh oi
þe bones.

Ne ȝe ne nan of heh lif þ̄
hone beo itempted. Oðer
beo ȝe gode þ̄ ar nel uben
hehe itempted þe þe yake. And tat
is resun. for se þe hul is herre of
hali lif ⁊ of heh· þa þe feondes
puffes· þe wind of fondiges ar in
strengre þron· ⁊ mare. Ȝif ani
ancker is þ̄ ne feleþ nane fon

diges· sinde dredeth point· þho
beo beo oð muchel toð sinde iston
ded· for þa sein Greg. seiþ. Tunc
maxime impugnaris cum te impug
nari nõ sentis. Sels mõ haues
tya estat sinde dred þule· þam is
hye· hene feles· nayt· his a hen sec
nesse· ⁊ for þi ne seches nayt ne
leache ne sea che craft· ne neal
kes na mõ read· ⁊ al te orues fer
liche ear mõ least· ȝene· his is te
ancker þ̄ nat noyt hyatis son
diges· to þeo se spekes· te engel ike
apocalipse· Dicis quia dlues sũ
et ulli· egeo· et nescis quia miser
es ⁊ pauiþ ⁊ cec̄· þus dis te nis ned
na medecine. Ah þu art blind
i herer ⁊ ni ne seist nayt· þu þuart
poure ⁊ naked of halinesse· ⁊
gastliche ⁊ wrecche· Þat oder dred
ful estat þ̄ te seke haues· is al stã
yard· ⁊ is· þis· hye he feles se much
el angoisse þ̄ he ne mai þoli enþ
mõ hodlen his sar· in þ̄ mõ hi hea
le þis is sum ancker þ̄ feles se

5. London, British Museum, Cotton MS. Titus D. xviii

'ANCRENE RIWLE' (English Text) (at fols. 14ʳ–105ʳ), a devotional manual of anonymous authorship composed in English about A.D. 1200 for a group of three anchoresses, subsequently revised and translated into French and Latin.

Written about A.D. 1225.

Vellum: 15·7 × 12·0 cm.

In a closely compressed book-hand.

Note. þ and ꝧ both used and still clearly differentiated; also ð is in use; note that 3 is written on the line (꟞) (cf. plate 4 also); in *a* the top bow is not yet meeting lower bowl; the 2-form of *r* used after *o* and rounded letters like ð; in *t* vertical only meets cross-bar (τ); *y* where used is dotted (ẏ) and ɩ bears a diacritic mark in form of an accent wherever ambiguity might occur.

Abbreviations are rare. Tironian nota for *and* is crossed now (ȝ). Note ꝧ for *þæt* and ' for omission of *er* (aft' = after).

In contractions the normal horizontal stroke is frequently replaced by a semicircular one (a characteristic feature of this scribe).

Correction is by dots below the relevant letters (cf. plate 3), e.g. 'beo', col. 2, line 2.

Text printed in: *The Ancren Riwle*, ed. J. Morton (Camden Soc., vol. lvii, 1853).

Another specimen in: Pal. Soc., ser. ii, pl. 75.

Our plate shows fol. 47ʳ.

TRANSCRIPTION

ꝧ mon seıs ıs sparepe uuel . Godd
hıt pıle for þı⫶ ꝧ ho beo eaù ead-
mod ȝ pıð lah haldınge of hı
reseluē falle dun to þe eorðe le-
ste ho prude . Nu pe hurten
leue chıldre to þe feorðe dale .
ꝧ ı seıde schulde beð of feole fon
dīges . for þer beð uttre ȝ ínre . ȝ
eıðer monı falde . Salue ıbıhet
to teachen to ȝeínes hā ȝ bote . And hu þase haues ham
meı Gederen of þıs dale con-
fort ȝ froure to ȝaínes ham
alle . Þat ıch þurh þe lare of
þe halı gast mote halde forep-
ard⫶ he hıt ȝeatı me þurh op-
re bones .

Ne pene nan of heh lıf ꝧ
ho ne beo ítēpted . Mare
beð þe gode ꝧ arn ıclūben
hehe ítēptet þē þe pake . And tat
ıs reısun . for se þe hul ıs herre of
halı lıf ȝ of heh⫶ spa þe feðdes
puffes . þe pínd of fondīges arn
strēgere þron . ȝ mare . ȝıf aní
anker ıs ꝧ ne feles nane fon

dīges⫶ spıðe drede ı ꝧ poínt . ꝧ ho
þẹọ beo où muchel ȝ où spıðe ıfon-
det . for spa seın Greg' seıs . Tunc
maxıme ımpugnarıs c̄ te īpug-
narı nō sentıs . Sek mō haues
tpa estat spıðe dredfule . ꝧ an ís
hpē he ne feles napt hıs ahen sec-
nesse . ȝ forþı ne seches napt ne
leache . ne leachecraft . ne ne as-
kes na mō read . ȝ asteorues fer-
lıche ear mō least pene . Þıs ıs te
anker ꝧ nat nopt hpat ıs fon-
dīge . To þeose spekes te engel ı þe
apocalıpse . Dıcıs quıa dıues sū
et nīlɩ egeo . et nescıs quıa mıser
es ȝ paup ȝ cec' . Þu seıs te nís ned
na medecíne . Ah þu art blínd
ıhertet . ní ne sest napt hu þu art
poure ȝ naked of halínesse . ȝ
Gastlıche precche . Þat oðer dredful estat ꝧ te seke haues⫶ ıs al frā-
pard tıs . ꝧ ıs hpē he feles se muchel angoısse . ꝧ he ne maı þolıen ꝧ
mō hōdlen hıs sar . ní ꝧ mō hī hea
le þıs ıs sum anker ꝧ feles se

5

6. London, British Museum, Cotton MS. Caligula A. ix

'BRUT' (at fols. 1ʳ–194ᵛ) composed by Laȝamon, a priest at *Ernleȝe* (probably Lower Arley or Arley Regis, near Bewdley, Worcestershire) perhaps between A.D. 1173 and A.D. 1207.

Written about A.D. 1250.[1]

Vellum: 21·5 × 15·7 cm.

The hand is now a well-marked Gothic book-hand, especially in its contrast of light and heavy strokes and emphasis on the latter, with a sharply compressed regularity, but still very rounded in character. Note as another characteristic the fusing of adjacent contrary curves as in *od, he,* &c., one of the most striking features of Gothic script. The letter-forms are now set in the shapes in which they will continue with a few modifications.

Note. t and c are well distinguished with the slightest

hint in some examples of the former of the vertical piercing the cross-bar; *s* and *t* are ligatured; the bow at the top of *a* is closing down on the lower bowl of the letter, an important detail for dating; in final positions round *s* is used; the 2-form of *r* is used after *o*; ð is still in use and ȝ is used (for *y-* as well as *g-* sound); insular or uncial *d* is employed throughout; *w* has taken the place of wyn (p) and þ has approximated in form to þ (wyn).

In abbreviations (rare) *and* is now (and will continue to be) indicated by Tironian nota in the form ⁊. Note the space-saving device of coalescing *h* and *t* in the writing of 'fulluht' in col. 1, l. 9 from foot.

Text printed in: *Laȝamon's Brut*, ed. F. Madden (London, 1847).

Another specimen in: New Pal. Soc., ser. i, pl. 86.

Our plate shows fol. 3ʳ (text, lines 1–98).

TRANSCRIPTION

Incipit hȳstoria brutonum .

AN preost wes on
leoden⫶ laȝamon
wes ihoten . He weˢ
leouenaðes sone⫶
liðe him beo drihtē
he wonede at ernleȝe⫶ at aðelen
are chirechen . vppen seuarne sta
þe⫶ sel þar him þuhte . On fest
Radestone⫶ þer he bock radde . Hit
com him on mode⫶ ⁊ on his Mern
þonke . þet he wolde of engle⫶ þa
æðelæn tellen . wat heo ihoten
weoren . ⁊ wonene heo comen .
þa englene londe ærest ahten .
æfter þan flode⫶ þe from drihtene
com þe al her aquelde quic þat
he funde . buten Noe . ⁊ semⁱ Japhet
⁊ cham . ⁊ heore four wiues⫶ þe mid
heom weren on archen . laȝamō
gon liðen ⫶ wide ȝond þas leode ⁊
biwon þa æðela boc⫶ þa he to bis
ne nom . he nom þa englisca boc ⫶
þa makede seint Beda . an oþer he
nom on latin⫶ þe makede seinte
albin⫶ ⁊ þe feire austin⫶ þe fulluħ
broute hider in . Boc he nom þe
þridde ⫶ leide þer amidden . þa ma
kede a frenchis clerc⫶ Wace wes
ihoten⫶ þe wel couþe writen . ⁊
he hoe ȝef þare æðelen⫶ alienor
þe wes henries quene⫶ þes heȝeˢ
kinges . Laȝamon leide þeos boc⫶
⁊ þa leaf wende . he heom leofliche

bi beold . liþe him beo drihten . fe
þeren he nom mid fingren⫶ ⁊ fie
de on boc felle . ⁊ þa soþ'e word⫶ set
te to gadere . ⁊ þa þre boc⫶ þrumde
to are . Nu bidded laȝamon alcne
aðele mon⫶ for þene almitē godd .
þet þeos boc rede⫶ ⁊ leornia þeos ru
nan . þ he þeos soð feste word . seg
ge to sumne . for his fader saule⫶
þa hine forð brouhte . ⁊ for his mo
der saule⫶ þa hine to monne iber .
⁊ for his awene saule ⫶ þat hire
þe selre beo . ameN .

Nv seið mid loft songe þe
wes on leoden preost . al
swa þe boc spekeð⫶ þe he
to bisne inom . Þa grickes hefdē
troȳe⫶ mid teone biwonē . ⁊ þ lond
iwest⫶ þa leoden of slawen · ⁊ for
þe wrake dome⫶ of Menelaus qᵉ
ne . and elene was ihoten . alðeodisc
wif . Þa paris alixandre⫶ mid pret
wrenche . bi won . for hire weoren
on ane daȝe⫶ hund þousunt deade .
vt of þan fehte⫶ þe was feondli
che stor . Eneas þe duc⫶ mid ermdē
at wond . Nefede he boten anne
sune⫶ þe was mid hím ifund .
asscaníus was ihoten⫶ nefede he
bern noma . ⁊ þes duc mid his drih
te⫶ to þare sa' hím droh . of kunne
⁊ of folke⫶ þe fulede þan duke . of
monne ⁊ of ahte⫶ þe he to þare
sæ brouhte . ⁊ tuenti gode scipen .

---

[1] This date is not in agreement with that usually cited (e.g. by New Pal. Soc., 'Early 13th Century'; J. Hall, *Selections*, ii, p. 450, 'written by two scribes in the first quarter of the Thirteenth Century'; B. Dickins and R. M. Wilson, *Early Middle English Texts*, p. 18, '*c.* 1225'), but I cannot persuade myself that this portion of the manuscript is other than about the *middle* of the century.

Incipit hystoria brutonum

An preost wes on
leoden· Laȝamon
wes ihoten· he wes
Leouenaðes sone·
liðe him beo drihte·
he wonede at ernleȝe· at æðelen
ire chirechen· vppen seuarne staþe·
sel þar him þuhte· on fest
radestone· þer he bock radde· þer
wunede on inone· & on his euen
ȝonke· þet he wolde of engle· þa
æðelæn tellen· wat heo ihoten
weoren· & wonene heo comen·
þa englene londe· ærest ahten·
æfter þan flode· þe from drihtene
com· þe al her aquelde quic þat
he funde· buten noe & sem· iaphet
cham· & heore four wiues· þe mid
heom weren on arken· Laȝamon
gon liðen wide ȝond þas leode· &
biwon þa æðela boc· þa he to bis
ne nom he nom þa englisca boc·
þa makede seint beda· an oðer he
nom on latin· þe makede seinte
albin· & þe feire austin· þe fulluht
brouhte hider in· boc he nom þe
þridde· leide þer amidden· þa makede
a frenchis clerc· wace wes
ihoten· þe wel couþe writen· &
he hoe ȝef þare æðelen· æliænor·
þe wes henries quene· þes heȝe
kinges· Laȝamon leide þeos boc·
þa leof him weren boc leofliche

bi leold· liðe him leo drihten· fe
seren he nom mid fingren· & fie
de on boc felle· & þa soþe word· fet
te togadere· & þa þre boc· þrumde
to are· nu bidded laȝamon alcne
æðele mon· for þene almiten godd·
þet þeos boc rede· & leornia þeos ru
nan· þat he þeos soðfeste word· seg
ge to summe· for his fader saule·
þa hine forð brouhte· & for his mo
der saule· þa hine to monne iber·
& for his awene saule· þat hire
þe selre beo· amen·

Þe seið and loft songr þe
wes oulend preost al
þa þe hir speked· þe be
to bisne mon· þa grickisc hefde
cruyse· and trowe bi wone· & filond
al werk· & þa leoden of crist en· & for
þe wurlie dome· of arcedauns c
nie· and elene wes ihoren· aldi de
wrf· þa pinus al wunder· and þas
wurteche· bi wone· for hine weoren
cruue duc· bend sunsure ac þe
ve of þan telirte· þe wes feondli
che þro· Incus þe duc· and ernde
at wond· Heffede he weren arde
sune· he wes and þen isund·
Samuel wes ihoren· neðra bi
arn noma· & þep ora ihl· con þe
te· to þere sæ þat him dol· þe bunne
r of solloe· þe fuled þa duke· of
norue & of aban· þe hi to sæu
er beoul er & frucurn gæt seipen

Ich was in one sumere dale.
In one suþe dizele hale.
Iherde ich holde grete tale.
an hule and one niztingale.
þat plait was stif & starc & strong.
sum wile softe & lud among.
an aiþer aзen oþer sval.
& let þat vole mod ut al.
& eiþer seide of oþeres custe.
þat alre worste þat hi wuste.
& hure & hure of oþere songe.
hi holde plaiding suþe stronge.
þe niztingale bigon þe speche.
in one hurne of one breche.
& sat vpone vaire boze.
þar were abute blosme inoze.
in ore vaste þicke hegge.
imeind mid spire & grene segge.
ho was þe gladur uor þe rise.
& song auele cunne wise.
het þuзte þe dreim þat he were.
of harpe & pipe þan he nere.
bet þuзte þat he were ishote.
of harpe & pipe þan of þrote.
þo stod on old stoc þarbiside.
þar þo vle song hure tide.
& was mid iui al bigrowe.
hit was þare hule eardingstowe.
þe niztingale hi iseз.
& hi biheold & oþerseз.
& þuзte wel vul of þare hule.
for me hi halt lodlich & fule.
vnu þu seist a wi þu flo.
aзe is þe bet þat ich þe so.

þis for þine vle lete.
wel oftriht mine song forlete.
miн horte atfliþ & falt miн tonge.
þonne þu art to me iþrunge.
me luste bet speten þane singe.
of þine fule зoзelinge.
þos hule abod fort hit was eve.
ho ne miзte no leng bileue.
for hure horte was so gret.
þat welneз hure fnast atset.
& warp a word þar aft longe.
hu þincþe nu bi mine songe.
wenst þu þat ich ne cunne singe.
þeз ich ne cunne of writelinge.
lom þu me dest me grame.
& seist me boþe tone & schame.
зif ich þe holde on mine vote.
so hit bitide þat ich mote.
& þu were vtof þine rise.
þu sholdest singe an oþer wise.

He niztingale зaf answare.
зif ich me loki wiþ þe bare.
& me schilde wiþ þe blete.
ne recche ich noзt of þine þrete.
зif ich me holde in mine hegge.
ne recche ich neuer what þu segge.
ich woт þat þu art un milde.
wiþ hom þat ne muзe fro þe schilde.
& þu tukest wroþe & vuele.
whar þu miзt over smale fuзele.
forþi þu art loþ al fuel kunne.
& alle ho þe driueþ honne.
& þe bi schricheþ & bi gredeþ.
& wel narewe þe bi ledeþ.

7. London, British Museum, Cotton MS. Caligula A. ix

'THE OWL AND THE NIGHTINGALE' (at fols. 233ʳ–246ʳ), composed probably about A.D. 1200 possibly but not certainly by Nicholas of Guildford.

Written probably a little after A.D. 1250.[1]

Vellum: 21·5 × 15·7 cm.

In a hand very closely related to that of Laȝamon, perhaps a little later, and with some peculiarities.

Note. þ (wyn) is still used but written with a point above, thus ṗ, and þ is written in þ form, the two being thus sharply differentiated[2]; ȝ is used for *gh*, and *y* and some *g* sounds; ð is used only in lines 902–60, 1184–end of poem and therefore does not appear in our plate; 2-form of *r* after *o*; tall *s* is normal, but round *s* at the end of words; in *t* the cross-bar is still not pierced by the vertical (ᴄ); *a* is now closed; there is a marked fusion of *dd, de, do.* d⋅ð

Tironian nota for *and* is in form ⁊.

Text printed in: *The Owl and the Nightingale*, ed. J. E. Wells (Boston and London, 1907, &c.); J. W. H. Atkins (Cambridge, 1922); and J. H. G. Grattan and G. F. H. Sykes (E.E.T.S., E.S., no. cxix, 1935).

Our plate shows fol. 233ʳ (text, lines 1–68).

TRANSCRIPTION

Ich ṗas ín one suṁe dale .
In one suþe [*sic* MS.] diȝele hale .
Iherde ich holde grete tale .
An hule and one niȝtingale .
Þat plait ṗas stif ⁊ starc ⁊ strõg .
Sum ṗile softe ⁊ lud among .
An asþer aȝen oþer sval .
⁊ let þat wole mod ut al .
⁊ eiþer seide of oþeres custe .
þat alẹre ṗorste þat hi ṗuste .
⁊ hure ⁊ hure of oþere songe .

Hi holde plaiding suþe stronge .
Þe niȝtingale bigon þe speche .
In one hurne of one broche .
⁊ sat upone vaire boȝe .
þar ṗere abute blosme ínoȝe .
In ore ṗaste þicke hegge .
I meínd mid spire ệ grene segge .
Ho ṗas þe gladur uor þe rise .
⁊ song auele cunne ṗíse .
Het þuȝte þe dreím þat he ṗere .
Of harpe ⁊ pipe þan he nere .
Bet þuȝte þat he ṗere ishote .
Of harpe ⁊ pipe þan of þrote .
þ o stod on old stoc þarbiside .
þar þo vle song hire tíde .
⁊ ṗas mid íuí albigroþe .
Hit ṗas þare hule eardingstoþe .
þ e niȝtingale hi iseȝ .
⁊ hi bihold ⁊ ouerseȝ .
⁊ þuȝte ṗel wl of þare hule .
For me hi halt lodlich ⁊ fule .
vn ṗiȝt ho sede a þei þu flo .
Me is þe wrs̲ þat ich þe so .

Iþis for þine wle lete .
ṗel oftích mine song forlete .
Min horte atfliþ ⁊ falt mi tonge .
þonne þu art to me iþrunge .
Me luste bet speten þane singe .

Of þine fule ȝoȝelínge .
ṗos hule abod fort hit ṗas [*sic* MS.] eve .
Ho ne miȝte no leng bileue .
vor híre horte ṗas so gret .
þat þelneȝ hire fnast at schet .
⁊ ṗarp a þord þar aft' longe .
Hu þincþe nu bi míne songe .
ṗest þu þat ich ne cunne sínge .
þeȝ ich ne cunne of þritelinge [*sic* MS.] .
Ilome þu dest me'gᵃme .
⁊ seist me boþe tone ⁊ schame .
ȝif ich þe holde on mine note .
So hit bitide þat ich mote .
⁊ þu ṗere vt of þíne rise .

þu sholdest sínge an oþer ṗ[i]se .
þe niȝtingale ȝaf answare .
ȝif ich me loki ṗit þe bare .
⁊ me schilde ṗit þe blete .
Ne reche ich noȝt of þíne þrete .
ȝif ich me holde in mine hegge .
Ne recche ich neù ṗhat þu segge .
Ich þot þat þu art un milde .
wiþ hom þat ne muȝe frõ se schilde .
⁊ þu tukest wroþe ⁊ vuele .
whar þu míȝt over smale fuȝele .
vorþi þu art loþ al fuel kunne .
⁊ alle ho þe dríueþ honne .
⁊ þe bi schricheþ ⁊ bigredet .
⁊ wel nareþe þe biledet .

NOT IN MS.

[1] This dating also differs from that normally assigned to the portion of the manuscript containing *The Owl and the Nightingale*, which I think is too early; Madden, op. cit. i, p. xxxv, writes of this part of the manuscript: 'The remaining portion of the volume [i.e. that containing *The Owl and the Nightingale*] was written at a later period, probably at the close of Henry the Third's reign', but this (i.e. towards A.D. 1272) is certainly too late, though even so probably nearer the mark than 'Early 13th century'.

[2] Close examination of the script will show that our scribe in fact uses slightly differing pen-strokes for his wyn and thorn; the two letters as written in his exemplar also sometimes caused him trouble—hence his three misreadings indicated in our passage.

"Wright's dating 'probably a little after A.D. 1250' seems to me a little on the early side." N. R. Ker Intro. to O&N EETS 251, p. ix.

8. London, British Museum, Arundel MS. 292

BESTIARY (at fols. 4–10ᵛ), composed possibly early in the thirteenth century, in East Midland dialect, the only extant Middle English version of the Bestiary.

Written about A.D. 1250–1300.

Vellum: 20·5 × 13·7 cm.

Book hand with court-hand flavour in details; similar in several general features to the hand in Stowe 34 (p. 3).

Note. A particularly odd form of ƿ is used (ƿ: made in three strokes); ð used throughout in place of þ; ð is close to slightly earlier court-hand form (ð); note the split tops of ascenders with hooks or spurs to left, thus ˀ| (cf. pl. 12) and well-marked curl to right in *h*; ȝ is not used at all, *g* being used for all *g*- and *y*-sounds; 2-form of *r* after *o*; and in *t* cross-bar is still not pierced by the vertical.

Tironian nota for *and* is ⁊.

Text printed in: *An Old English Miscellany*, ed. R. Morris (E.E.T.S., o.s., no. 49, 1872, pp. 1–25).

Our plate shows fol. 4ʳ (text, lines 1–59).

TRANSCRIPTION

Ðe leun stant on hılle . ⁊ he man hunten **Nat'a leōıs . ıᵃ .**
here . Oðer ðurg hıs nese smel . Smake ðat he negge . Bı
ƿılc ƿeıe so he ƿıle . To dele nıðer ƿenden . Alle hıse fet step-
pes . After hím he filleð . Drageð dust ƿıð hıs stert . ðer he
steppeð . Oðer dust oðer deu . ðat he ne cunne ıs finden . drí-
ueð dun to hıs den . ðar he hím bergen ƿılle . **ıȷᵃ**——
An oðer kínde he haueð . ƿanne he ıs ıkındled . Stılle lıð
ðe leun . ne stıreð he nout of slepe . Tıl ðe sunne haueð
sínen ðrıes hím abuten . ðanne reıseð hıs fader hím .
mıt te rem ðat he makeð . **iıȷᵃ** .——————
Ðe ðrıdde lage haueð ðe leun . ðanne he lıeð to slepen .
Sal he neure luken . ðe lıdes of hıse egen . **sıgnıficacō**
Ƿelle heg ıs tot hıl . ðat ıs heuen rıche . Vre **ƿᶦme nat^ᵅe** .
louerd ıs te leun . ðe líueð ðer abuuen . ƿu ðo hım lıke-
de . to lıgten her on erðe . Mıgte neure díuel ƿıten . ðog he
be derne hunte . hu he dun come . Ne ƿu he dennede hım
ín ðat defte meıden . Marıe bı name . ðe hım lar to man-
ne frame . Ðo ure drıgten ded ƿas . ⁊ doluen also hıs . **ıȷᵃ** . . ⁊ **ııȷᵃ** .
ƿılle ƿas . In a ston stılle he laı . tıl ıt kam ðe drıdde daı .
Hıs fader hım filstnede spo . ðat he ros fro dede ðo . Vs to
lıf holden . ƿakeð so hıs ƿılle ıs So hırde for hıs folde . he
ıs hırde . ƿe ben sep . Sılden he us ƿılle . If ƿe heren to hıs
ƿord . ðat ƿe ne gon noƿor ƿılle . **Natura aquıle** .——————
Kıðen ı ƿılle ðe ernes kínde . Also ıc ıt o boke rede . ƿu he
neƿeð hıs guðhede . Hu he turneð ut of elde . Sıðen hıse
lımes arn unƿelde . Sıðen hıs bec ıs alto ƿrong . Sıðen hıs

e leun stant on hille · = he man hunten
here · oðer ðurg his nese smel · smake ðat he negge · bi
wilc weie so he wile · to dele nider wenden · Alle hise fet step
pes · after him he filleð · Drageð dust wið his stert · ðer he
steppeð · Oðer dust oðer deu · ðat he ne cunne is finden · dri
ueð dun to his den · ðar he him bergen wille.

An oðer kinde he haueð · þanne he is skindled stille lið
ðe leun · ne stireð he nout of slepe · til ðe sunne haueð
þinen þries him abuten · ðanne reiseð his fader him ·
mid te rem ðat he makeð.

Þe ðridde lage haueð ðe leun · ðanne he lieð to slepen ·
sal he neure luken · ðe lides of hise egen ·

elle beg is ðat þil · ðat is heuen riche · lure
louerd is te leun · ðe liueð ðer abuuen · þu to him like
ðe · to ligten her on erðe · Hirgte neure diuen þten · ðog he
ðederne hunne · hu he dun come · He þu he ðennede him
in ðat deste merðen · Harue bi name · ðe him lat to man
ne frame · Do ure drigten ded was · & doluen also his
wille was · in a ston stille he lai · til it kam ðe ðridde dai ·
his fader him filstnede swo · ðat he ros fro dede to · þl to
lif holden · þaked so his wille is · so hude for his fofte · he
is hude · þe ben sep · siden he is wtte · if þe heuen to his
word · ðat þe ne gon noþor wille ·

iden i wille ðe ernes kinde · Also re it o boke rede · þu he
neweð his gudhede · hu he tunneð ut of elde · siden his te
luues ar n unfelde · siden his tee it alro þronge · siden his

Lenten ys come wiþ love to toune,
Wiþ blosmen & wiþ briddes roune,
þat al þis blisse bryngeþ.
Dayeʒes eʒes in þis dales,
Notes suete of nyhtegales,
Vch foul song singeþ.
þe þrestelcoc him þreteþ oo;
Away is huere wynter wo
When woderone syngeþ.
þis foules singeþ ferly fele,
Ant wlyteþ on huere wynter wele,
þat al þe wode ryngeþ.

þe rose rayleþ hire rode;
þe leues on þe lyhte wode
Waxen al wiþ wille.
þe mone mandeþ hire bleo,
þe lilie is lossom to seo,
þe fenyl & þe fille.
Wowes þis wilde drakes,
Miles murgeþ huere makes,
Ase strem þat strikeþ stille.
Mody meneþ so doþ mo;
Ichot ycham on of þo,
for loue þat likes ille.

þe mone mandeþ hire lyht,
So doþ þe semly sonne bryht,
When briddes singeþ breme.
Deawes donkeþ þe dounes,
Deores wiþ huere derne rounes,
Domes forte deme.
Wormes woweþ vnder cloude,
Wymmen waxeþ wounder proude,
So wel hit wol hem seme.
ʒef me shal wonte wille of on,
þis wunne weole y wole forgon
Ant wyht in wode be fleme.

In maþhit mungeþ when hit dawes
An donneʒ deawes wiþ his dueʒes plawes
An lef is lyht on lynde.
Blosmes bredeþ on þe bowes,
Al þis wylde wyhtes wowes,
So wel þeh wonder fynde.
Ynot non so freoli flour
Ase ledies þat beþ bryht in bour,
Wiþ loue who mihte hem bynde.
So worþly wymmen are by west,
One of hem ich herie best,
from Irlond in to ynde.

Wymmen were þe beste þing
þat shup oure heʒe heuene kyng
ʒef feole false nere.
Heo beoþ so lad vpon huere ʒed
To loue þer me hem laste bed,
When heo shule þenge fere.
Lut in londe aʒe to leue,
þah me hem trewe troweþe ʒeue,
for þherie so ʒeuy.
When trichour haþ is troube yplyht,
Biswyken he haþ þat suete wyht
þah he hire oþes sweye.
Wymmen war þe wiþ þe swike
þat feir ant froely ys to fyke,
þis sawe is o to fonde.
So þude in worlde þer huere wone,
In vch a toune vntyde wiþ is on,
from Bonecestre to Lounde.
of trewe loue ne þenke riht nohte,
bote he habbe is wille ywroht,
At stevenyng vmbestounde.
Ah feire leuedis be on war
To late comeþ þe ʒeyn char,
When loue ou haþ ybounde.

9. London, British Museum, Harley MS. 2253

'HARLEY LYRICS', a collection of English secular lyrics, so called from their preservation (with other material, e.g. King Horn, in French, English, and Latin) in this MS. (at fols. 49ʳ–140ʳ *passim*), written in West Midland dialect (the MS. coming without doubt from Leominster Priory).[1]

Written probably between A.D. 1314 and A.D. 1325 (a reference to the Battle of Bannockburn, A.D. 1314, occurs in a Thomas of Erceldoune prophecy, fol. 127ʳ).

Vellum: 29·5 × 19 cm.

Written in a court-hand similar to that used in the charters of the period and found also in French and English literary texts in other contemporary MSS., e.g. the Brut poem in Brit. Mus. Royal MS. 12 C. xii (fols. 62ʳ–68ᵛ) and in the Fulk Fitz-Warin romance in the same MS. (fols. 33ʳ–60) (cf. *Catalogue of Royal MSS.* iv, plate 69), with the cursive flourishes characteristic of the non-book-hand.

Note. Note the elaboration of þ, w (wyn (ƿ) has disappeared), long s in initial positions, and d; note in g the flattening of the tail (ᵹ) (and cf. similar g in Royal MS. referred to above); upper bow of a (closed) is brought well above the mid-line; final s is of Greek type (σ); the 2-form of r does not appear; i has usually a slanting stroke over it; y is sometimes dotted; the y-sound (as in ȝere) and hard g-sound are represented by ȝ and g respectively, the former being also utilized for s and z in French loanwords; th is usually represented by þ (ð is never used) but sometimes th is written out; u is used for consonant and vowel.

In abbreviation *and* is represented by the Tironian nota in a cursive form (as in contemporary court-hand) ⁊, and *er* is indicated by '.

Text printed in: K. Böddeker, *Altenglische Dichtungen des MS. Harl. 2253* (Berlin, 1878), and *The Harley Lyrics*, ed. G. L. Brook (Manchester, 1948).

Other specimens in: Brook, op. cit., frontispiece, and New Pal. Soc., ser. ii, pl. 241.

Our plate shows fol. 71ᵛ.

TRANSCRIPTION

¶ Lenten ẏs come wiþ loue to toune
  wiþ blosmen ⁊ wiþ briddes roune
  þᵗ al þis blisse brýngeþ
  daẏes eȝes in þis dales
  notes suete of nẏhtegales
  vch foul song síngeþ
  þe þrestelcoc him þreteþ oo
  away ís huere wynter wo
  when woderoue spᵒngeþ.
  þis foules singeþ ferly fele
  ant wlyteþ on huere wynter wele
  þat al þe wode rýngeþ
  þe rose raẏleþ hire rode
  þe leues on þe lyhte wode
  waxen al wíþ wille
  þe mone mandeþ hire bleo
  þe lilie ís lossom to seo
  þe fenýl ⁊ þe fille
  wowes þis wilde drakes
  miles murgeþ huere makes
  ase strem þᵗ stᵗkeþ stílle
  modý meneþ so doh moᵒ
  ȷchot ẏcham on of þoᵒ
  for loue þᵗ likes illeᵒ
  þe mone mandeþ hire lyht
  so doþ þe semly sonne brýht
  when briddes singeþ breme
  deawes donkeþ þe dounes
  deores wíþ huere derne rounes
  domes forte demeᵒ
  wormes woweþ vnder cloude
  wymmen waxeþ wounder proude
  so wel hit wol heme seme
  ȝef me shal wonte wille of on
  þis wunne weole ẏ wole forgon
  ant wyht in wode be fleme

¶ In maẏ hit murgeþ when hit dawes
  ȷn dounes wiþ þis dueres plawes
  ant lef is lyht on lynde
  blosmes bredeþ on þe bowes
  al þis wýlde wyhtes wowes
  so wel ych vnderfýnde
  ynot non so freoli flour
  ase ledíes þᵗ beþ bryht ín bour
  wiþ loue who míhte hem býnde
  so worlý wýmmen are bý west
  one of hem ich heríe best
  from ȷrlond in to ýnde
  wymmen were þe beste þing
  þᵗ shup oure heȝe heuene kyng
  ȝef feole false nere
  heo beoþ to rad vpon huere redᵒ
  to loue þer me hem lastes bed
  when heo shule fenge fereᵒ
  Lut in londe are to leue
  þah me hem trewe trouþe ȝeueᵒ
  for tᵗcheríe to ȝere
  when tᵗchour haþ ís trouþe ýplyht
  býswýken he haþ þᵗ suete wyht
  þah he híre oþes swere
  wýmmon war þe wiþ þe swyke
  þat feír ant freolý ẏs to syke
  ẏs fare ís o to founde
  so wyde ín world ys huere won
  ín vch a toune vntrewe ís on
  from Leycestre to Loundeᵒ
  of treuþe nís þe tᵗchour noht
  bote he habbe ís wille ẏwroht
  at steuenýng vmbe stoundeᵒ
  ah feyre leuedis be on war
  to late comeþ þe ȝeyn char
  when loue on haþ ýbounde

[1] Note the legend of St. Etfrid (ff. 132–3) which, as Joseph Hall (*King Horn*, Oxford, 1901, p. viii) points out, represents a purely local tradition, that of the priory's alleged foundation in the seventh century. It is to be observed too that in the MS. at the head of the legend is a very prominent red cross.

10. London, British Museum, Cotton MS. Caligula A. xi

CHRONICLE OF ROBERT OF GLOU-CESTER (at fols. 3–168ʳ): composed originally in the Gloucester dialect, the work of probably three authors, viz. A, a monk of Gloucester Abbey who late in the thirteenth century composed a metrical history of Britain to the death of Henry I; B, a monk of the same house, named Robert, who shortly after A.D. 1297 wrote a recension of A, adding 3,000 lines to the story to bring it down to the end of Henry III's reign; C, also a Gloucester monk, who wrote up A in a shorter version. The present MS. is the earliest of the longer version by B.

Written between about A.D. 1300 and A.D. 1325.

Vellum: 22·5 × 15·5 cm.
Roughly of the same date as the 'Harley Lyrics' MS. but written in a book-hand.

Note. Normally *a* is practically closed in its top bow, sometimes completely; the þ is now written in the 'wyn'-form; wyn itself is displaced by *w*; 2-form of *r* used after *o*; 3 is used for *y*-sound (3onge), *gh* (fi3te), &c., and for *z* (and *tz*-sound, as in 'fi3Jon') (see Intro., § 2 and for references p. xv, n. 2); both forms of *s* appear; the vertical of *t* is just above the cross-bar; *i* is usually distinguished by a fine slanting hair stroke; minims of *m* and *n* are now connected by fine hair lines; *y* is dotted.

Contractions are infrequent: note, however, þᶜ (instead of þ) for *þæt*, þ' for *þer*. Tironian nota for *and* is ⁊.

Text printed in: *The Metrical Chronicle of Robert of Gloucester*, ed. W. A. Wright (Rolls Series, no. 86, London, 1887).

Our plate shows fol. 165ʳ (text, lines 11746–83).

TRANSCRIPTION

. Henric' .

An vewe dropes of reíne . þer velle grete ínou .
þís toknínge vel ín þís lond . þo me þís men slou .
vor þrettí míle þanne . þís íseí roberd .
þat verst þís boc made . ⁊ was wel sore aferd .
⁊Loùdínges þ' were ínome . at euesham maníon .
as sír unfraí de boun . Sír Jon le fí3 Jon .
⁊ símondes sone . de moūtfort sır gwẏ .
sír baudewíne de wake . sír Jon de vescẏ .
sír henrí de hastínges . ⁊ sır Nícole íwís .
De se3ue was þere ínome . ⁊ al so sír perís .
⁊ sír roberd þat sír perís . de moūtfort sones were .
þuse ⁊ wel mo were ínome . ⁊̄ þulke morþre þere .
⁊Ac þe welsse fot men . þat þer were maníon .
ac þe bígínnínge of þe bataıle . bígonne to fle echon .
⁊ come þoru teuskesburí . ⁊ þere men of þe toune .
Slowe hom al to groūde . þat þere híí leíe þ' doune
so þícke bístrete . þat reuþe ít was to se .
⁊ grace nadde non of hom . to fí3te ne to fle .
⁊þo þe bataıle was ído . ⁊ þe godemen aslawe were .
sir símond þe 3onge com . to mete ís fad' þere .
he mí3te þo at ís díner . abbe bıleued al so wel .
as me seíþ wan ích am ded . make me a caudel .
⁊ þo me tolde hím bí þe weí . wuch þe ende was þer .
he turnde a3en to keníngwurþe . wel longe hím þou3te e[r]
he mí3te segge wan he com . lute ích abbe ıwonne .
Ich maí honge vp mín ax . feblıche î abbe agonne
⁊þe kíng of alemaıne . þat was ís moder broþer .
⁊ sír reínaud le fí3 perís . ⁊ ek maní anoþer .
þat ín ís p'son were . at kenígwurþe þo .
þo he ne seí oþ' red . he let hom quít go .
þe síxte daẏ of septembre . þat þo was sonendaẏ .
he let hom go a godes half . þo he oþer ne saẏ .
þe kíng þo3te þe loundreís . brínge al to nou3te .
⁊ híí ofte pítoslıche . ís grace bí sou3te .
So þᵗ at mísselmasse . an fourtí of hom come .
To hím to wíndelsore . ⁊ to ís grace hom nome .
As vor al þe toune . þe beste íchose echon .
þe kíng hom let brínge . ín strong p'son anon .

10

a n belße dropes of reine. per belle grete mou.
þ is toknuige vel in þis loud. po me þis men slou.
v oa prein mile paine. þis iþel robeud
þ at berst þis boc made. t was bel sore afeud.
L oudriges þ were inome. at euesham manion.
a s sir bufrai de boun. sir þon le fiz þon.
t simondes sone. de montfort s ir gilþi.
s ir baudelbine de bahe. sir þon de vesty.
s ir henri de hastinges. t sir Nicole ilais.
b e segue was þere inome. t al so sir peris.
t sir robeud þat sir peris. de montfort sones were.
þ use t bel mo bere inome. t þulke morþre þere.
a c þe belþe fot men. þat þer were manion
a c þe biginnuige of þe bataile. bigonne to fle echou
t come þam teuskesburi. t þere men of þe toune.
S tolbe hom al to groude. þat þere hu leie þ doune
þo þicke bistrete. þat reuþe it bas to se.
t grace nadde non of hom. to fizte ne to fle.
þ o þe bataile bas ido. t þe godemen aslabe were.
s ir simond þe zonge com. to mete is fad þere
h e mizte þo at is diner. abbe bileued al so bel.
a s me seiþ ban ich am ded. make me a caudel.
t þo me tolde hym bi þe bei. þuch þe eude bas þer.
h e turude azen to keuingburþe. bel longe hym þouzte
h e mizte segge ban he com. litte ich abbe ibonne.
J ch mai honge vp miu ax. febliche I abbe agonne
þ e king of allemaine. þat bas is moder broþer.
t sir remaud le fiz peris. t ek mam an oþer.
þ at in is þson bere. at keuigburþe þo.
þ o he ne sei oþ red. he let hom quit go.
þ e sire dai of septembre. þat þo bas sonendai.
h e let hom go a godes half. þo he oþer ne sai.
þ e king þozte þe loudreis. bringe al to nouzte.
t hi ofte priosliche. is grace bi þizte.
S o þ at miþelmasse. au fourti of hom come.
T o hiu to bindelfoue. t to is grace hom nome.
a s vor al þe toune. þe bette ichoþe echou.
þ e king hom let bringe in stronge þson anan.

In ye first he com tempt to be
ye toþer demster self sal he
O þis come sal be takens sere
Befor cumand þt ye sal here
Witvten þt þese allwais
As risand mare o gret vp pain
ffor qm of all þar sal an rise
þat cristen mast sal do grise
þt al þis werld o length and brede
sal send his wickednes to sprede
þt antiþ o dauis sede
Sum thing of him es for to rede
þe þt sua fild o goddis gram
Qvarfor he sal ha snilk a nam
ffor þi es he cald Antecrist
ffor he sal be gains ihu crist
agains crist þt es to sai
ffor gain his werc he sal werrai
Crist come meke al in his tide
he sal cume reth raisand in pride
Crist come at do ye tagh to rais
ye sinful for to mak rightwise
Bot he sal tru ye meke to fell

And o þe kind man clepes dauc
þt prophet mas o vus his nam
Whne he sais neder in strete
to do ye rider fall bi þe wai
þt als mikel es for to sai
bi þe wai als nedder sal he sitt
þt all yai men þt he mai witt
fidand in ye reule o right
he sal yam smett and dun ya light
he sal yam giue ful attre dint
vte of yair trouth yam for to stint
O fader and mod he sal be born
als oþer men es him bi forn
Bituix a man and a woman
And noght of a maiden allan
Als it es foli tald o sum
sloght tun a bisshop and a nu
Bot of bismer brein and bald
And geten of a glotun scald
yat yar mai be na fuler tun
he sal begeten al in sin
Geten in sin and born in plight

11. London, British Museum, Cotton MS. Vespasian A. iii

'CURSOR MUNDI', a metrical encyclopedia of Biblical study, composed about A.D. 1300–1325 in the north.

Written about A.D. 1340.

Vellum: 23 × 16·5 cm.

In a round heavy characteristic 14th-century hand.

Note. þ discontinued and *w* always used now, and þ is in *y*-form; *s* appears in both long and round forms; 2-form of *r* is used after *o* and some other rounded letters (e.g. *b*); *i* has fine hair stroke, which is important in words made up of minims (e.g. 'min'); *a* with its closed bow is now like an angular 8; ʒ is not used, *g* being normal; note fusion of *do, de.*

Abbreviations are rare—the usual horizontal stroke has ticks at end (˥); for *þæt* þᵗ is used and for *er* ' (e.g. 'mod'').

Text printed in: *The 'Cursor Mundi'*, ed. R. Morris (E.E.T.S., o.s., nos. 57, 59, 62, 66, 68, 99, 1874–92).

Our plate shows fol. 123ᵛ (upper half only) (text lines 21965–87, 22011–33).

TRANSCRIPTION

In þe first he com dempt to be
þe toþer demster self sal he
☉ þis come sal be takens sere
Befor cūmand þᵗ ye sal here
witvten þᵗ we se alwais
Aı rısand mare o gret vp pais
ffor quı of all þar sal an rise
þat cristen mast sal do grise
þᵗ al þıs werld o length and brede
sal send his wickednes to sprede
þᵗ antıχᵗ o danıs sede
Sū thing of him es for to rede
he þᵗ sua fild o godds gram
Quarfor he sal ha squılk anam
ffor þı es he cald antıcrıst
ffor he sal be ganıs ıhù crıst
Agaıns crıst þᵗ es to saı
ffor gaın his werc he sal werraı
Crıst come meke al ın his tıde
he sal cūme reth raısand ın pıde
Crıst come at do þe lagh to raıs
þe sınful for to mak rıght wıse
Bot he sal cū þe meke to fell

and o þe kınd man clepes dane
þᵗ pphet mas o þus his nam
Dane he saıs neder ın strete
waıtand hors to stang ín fete
to do þe rıder fall bı þe waı
þᵗ als mıkel es for to saı
Bı þe waı als nedder sal he sıtt
þᵗ all þaa men þᵗ he maı wıjt
Rıdand ın þe reule o rıght
he sal þam smett and dun þā lıght
he sal þam gıue ful attre dınt
vte of þaír trouth þam for to stínt
¶☉ fader and mod' he sal be born
als oþer men es hím bıforn
Bıtuıx a man and a wōman
and noght of a maıden allan
als ıt es folı tald o sum
Noght tuíx a bıscop and a nū
Bot of bısmer brem and bald
and geten of a glotun scald
þat þar maı be na fuler tuín
he sal be geten al ın sín
Geten ín sín and born ín plıght

'AYENBITE OF INWYT' (at fols. 13ʳ–96ʳ), the translation of Friar Lorens' 'Le Somme des Vices et des Vertues' by Michael of Northgate, a monk of St. Augustine's Abbey, Canterbury.

Written A.D. 1340 (see fol. 4ʳ), the *autograph* MS.

Vellum: 31 × 20·5 cm.

In a vigorously written script, basically book-hand but without its self-conscious formality.

Note. ʒ is used for *gh*-sound ('almiʒti') and *w*-sound (laʒe) (not for *y*-sound which is represented by *y*); hard *g* is represented by *g* and *th* by a properly made þ; *w* always, þ never; *y* is dotted and *i* has nearly always a slanting stroke; 2-form of *r* used after *o*; both long and round *s* used (and note the frequent use of *z* for initial *s*, a dialectal feature shared with the south-west); note very elaborate *a*, the top bow carried exaggeratedly above the line and then brought down to touch the lower bowl; ascenders of *l*, &c., have the appearance of being wedge-shaped at top, the wedge usually being split (an effect due to the addition of a sort of spur or quirk at the top left-hand side of the ascender; cf. also plate 8).

Text printed in: *Dan Michel's Ayenbite of Inwyt*, ed. R. Morris (E.E.T.S., o.s., no. 23, 1866).

Another specimen in: Pal. Soc., ser. i, pl. 197.

Our plate shows fol. 13ʳ (upper half only).

TRANSCRIPTION

. I .

. þe uore speche .

Almiʒti god ẏaf ten hestes íne þe laʒe of íewes | þet Moẏses onderníng | íne þe helle of Sẏnaẏ | íne tuo tables of ston | þet were íwríte | míd godes víngre͘ . And hím zelf | efter hıs berīge | íne hís spelle | het híse healde | and lokı | to ech man | þet wıle bẏ ẏborʒe . And huo þet agelt | íne eníe of þe ılke hestes: hím ssel þerof uor͘ þenche | and hím ssríue | and bıdde god me̜cí | ẏef he wẏle bẏ ẏborʒe . Þís boc ís ẏwríte | uor englísse men þet hí wẏte | hou hí ssolle ham zelue ssrí͘ ue | and makı ham klene | íne þíse líue . Þís boc hatte huo þet wrít | aẏenbíte of ínwẏt . Auerst bẏeþ þe hestes ten | þet lokí ssolle alle men . ⊂ þe uerste

Þe uerste heste þet god made | and het: ís þís . þou ‖ *godes heste* . ne sselt habbe | uele godes . þet ıs to zígge | þou ne sselt habbe god bote me . ne worssípíe | ne seru̜. And þou ne sselt do þíne hope | bote íne me . Vor þe ılke | þet deþ hís hope | heʒlíche íne sseppe: zeneʒeþ dẏadlíche . and deþ aẏe þíse heste . Zuíche bẏeþ þe ılke | þet worssípeþ þe momenes . and makeþ híre god | of sseppe | huích þet hít bẏ . Aẏe þíse heste | zeneʒeþ þo | þet to moche | louíeþ híre guod . gold . oþer zeluer . oþer oþre þíges | erþlíche . Huo þet | íne þíse þínges agelteþ: zetteþ zuo moche híre herte | and híre hope : þet hí uorẏeteþ | híre sseppere . an leteþ hím | þet alle þíse guodes ham leuþ . And þeruore | hí ssolden hím seruí | and þonkı | and toppe alle þínges | louíe | and worssípíe | alzuo þe tekþ | þís uerste heste . ⊂ þe oþer

Þe oþer heste | ẏs þelhch . þou ne sselt níme | godes name : ‖ *godes heste* . ín ẏdel . þet ís to zígge : þou ne sselt zueríe | uor naʒt | and wẏþ ou͘

Al þat he fonde wtinne house
þys dingu ologh to merueylouse
So moche folke gan he quelle
wen seyd he was a fende of helle
Alle þe folk of þat citte
Cunseyled he what þat myȝti be
þey armyde he alle at here myȝtt
Aȝenȝ þe dingu for to fyȝtt
But non of hem myȝti vndyrstande
Wher þe dragu was wonande
Befel it þat yche tyde
An ermyte wonede þer besyde
A gode man and wyȝt certeyn
Disselled þat wasteyn besyde
One of he ȝaf tuȝyl tyte
þat þey schulde go to þat ermyte
And aske tuȝyl of osbyche a sede
In hope alle þe bettyr to spede
Whan þey hadde tolde hy alle her dere
þys was þan þe crayryȝt answere
ȝyf ȝe wyl were for ȝour synne
And chyrue ȝow clene & þof blynne
And graunte me þat ȝe schul faste
And yn preyers wel to laste
Penuentyue ȝe may be aleggys
And so of sprowȝ abreggys
To do alle þe ermyte bad
þey grauntede alle & wer ryȝt glad
þe ermyte seyde ȝe schul be
In penaunce þre days wtme
And aftyr þe presayȝt ȝ ende
To ȝow schal y come or sende
Alle went home þer weye
þe ermyte hys preyer began to seye
Ihu cryst god almyȝtty
Of þys folk haue þou mercy
þat þou boȝttyȝt on rode to dere
For he schewe me on tu manere

Where y may þe dragu fynde
And hys power bynde
þat þe folk may knowe and se
þe mercy and þe myȝt of þe
Whan he hadde preyde hys crysti
sone yn grete afflyctyu
for caȝt alle hys entent
And hys aungel to hy he sent
for to teche hy þe way
þe syr þer þe dragu lay
þe aungel seyd to þe ermyte
Do sumne þe folk astyte
þat þey come alle hedyr
before þe echone to gedyr
y chal be ȝour alyȝer leder
þat þe dragu ȝow natt dere
þe folk echone þedyr com
þe aungel before he gan gon
And lede he to þat wasteyn
þat su tyme was a stede certeyn
Vnto a place þey ȝede echone
And þer þey fonde a tumbe of stone
þe aungel bad he lyfte vp þe lydde
And as he bad ryȝt so þey dydde
her he seyde ys hys wonnyng
W'anoþ wykked þyng
þese ȝow noȝtt port he be folunde
for al hys power haue y bounde
Wha þey had þe toumbe otbrymne
þe folk stode and lokede wtynne
þey caȝt a woman þere wyly lye
And her body cloue yn þrey partye
Betwyȝe þo þrey partys þe body lay
firstly to se wt grete affray
Grete wndyr was hyt to se
þey askede alle what hyt myȝt be
And why hyt was and wher fore
þat þe dragu lay so þore

13. London, British Museum, Harley MS. 1701

'HANDLYNG SYNNE' (at fols. 1ʳ–84ʳ), an adaptation by Robert Mannyng of Bourne, Lincolnshire (born about A.D. 1283) of William of Waddington's 'Manuel des Péchiez'.

Written about A.D. 1380.

Vellum: 28·5 × 20·7 cm.

The hand is suggestive in general character of that of the Piers Plowman C-Text MS., Cotton Vespasian B. xvi (pl. 14).

Note. 3 is used for the *gh* and *y*-sounds; þ is used, but not ƿ (always *w*); in *t* the vertical is only just above the cross-bar; for *s* the round form is used for capitals (S), otherwise the long *s* and Greek *s* (σ); in the combination *gh* note that *h* has a horizontal stroke through ascender (għ); the 2-form of *r* used after *o* has now usually a tag (thus ɿ); *y* is sometimes dotted; note the absence of *i*.

Abbreviations are simple: wᵗ for *with* and ' for final *e* and *er* (e.g. her', neu' for *here, neuer*).

Text printed in: *Robert of Brunne's Handlyng Synne*, ed. F. J. Furnivall (E.E.T.S., o.s., nos. 119, 123, 1901, 1903).

Our plate shows fol. 12ᵛ (text, lines 1751–1826).

TRANSCRIPTION

The syxte comaūdemēt ys
Al þat he fonde wᵗoute house
Þys dragū slogħ so merueylouse
So moche folke gan he quelle
Men seyd he was a fende of helle
Alle þe folk of þat cūtre
Cunseyled hē ? what þat mygħt be
Þey armyde hē alle at here mygħt
A3ens þe dragū for to fygħt
But noū of hem mygħt vndyrstande
Wher' þe dragū was wonande
Befel 3yt þat ẏche tẏde
An ermyte wonede þer' besyde
A gode man and ry3t certeyn
Dwelled ‖ þat wasteyn ‖ besyde ‖
One of hē 3af cūseyl tyte
þat þey shulde go to þat Ermyte
And aske cūseyl of swyche a dede
In hope alle þe bettyr to spede
Whā þey hadde tolde hȳ alle her' dere
Þys was þan þe ermytys answere
3yf 3e wyl wepe' for 3our' synne
And shryue 3ow clene ē þ' of blynne
And graūte me þat 3e shul faste
And yn preyers wel to laste
Perauenture 3e may be aleggyd
           3oure
And sū of ∧ sorow abreggyd
           þat
To do alle ∧ þe ermyte bad
Þey graūtede alle ē wer' ry3t glad
Þe ermyte seyde 3e shul be
In penaūce þre days wᵗ me
And aftyr þe þre days ende
To 3ow shal y . come or sende
‖ þe folk Alle ‖ went home þer' weye
þe ermyte hys preyer' began to seye
Ihū crẏst god almygħty
Of þys folk haue þou mercẏ
þat þou bogħtyst on rode so dere
ffor hē shewe me on sū manere

þou shalt no hordam do
Where y . may þe dragū fynde
And hys power lorde þou bynde
þat þe folk may knowe and se
þe mercẏ and þe my3t of þe
Whan he hadde preyde hys orysū
Long yn grete afflyctyū
God sagħ alle hys entent
And hys aūgel to hȳ he sent
ffor to teche hȳ þe way
þedyr þer' þe dragū laẏ
þe aūgel seyd to þe ermyte
Do sumne þe folk astyte
þat þey come alle hedyr
Before þe echone togedẏr
ẏ shal be 3our' alþer ledere
                      desese.
þat þe dragū 3ow nat dere
þe folk echone þedyr com
þe aūgel before hē gan gon
And led hē to þat wasteyn
þat sū tyme was a stede certeyn
Vnto a place þey 3ede echone
And þer' þey fonde a tumbe of stone
þe aūgel bad hē lyft vp þe lydde
And as he bad ry3t so þey dydde
Her' he seyde ys hys wonnyng
Wᵗ a noþ' wykked þyng
Drede 3ow nogħt þo3t he be fownde
ffor al hys power haue y bownde
Whā þey had þe toumbe . o . twynne
þe folk stode and loked wᵗ ynne
þey sagħ a wōman þere vyly lye
And her' bodẏ cloue yn twey partye
Betwyxe þo tweẏ partys þe bodẏ laẏ
Greslẏ to se wᵗ grete affraẏ
Grete wndyr was hyt to see
þey asked alle what hyt my3t be
And whẏ hyt was and wher' fore
Þat þe dragū laẏ so þore

13

14. London, British Museum, Cotton MS. Vespasian B. xvi

'THE VISION OF PIERS PLOWMAN', by William Langland (at fols. 6ʳ–95ʳ), the C-Text (or third edition), which may have been composed about A.D. 1393–8.

Written not later than A.D. 1400.

Vellum: 26·5 × 18 cm.

Strongly influenced by court-hand: Pal. Soc. editors note MS. as 'still preserving the round style characteristic of the 14th century'.

Note. þ has lost the top of its ascender and would be indistinguishable from ƿ if the latter were still being used; ȝ is still used for *y*-sound, *gh*-sound, &c.; the vertical of the *t* is brought just above the cross-bar, and *c* and *t* are liable to confusion; the 2-form of *r* is used consistently after *o* but also sometimes after other (rounded) letters (e.g. *d*); *y* is dotted and the *i* where it might be ambiguous has a slanting stroke (e.g. in 'him') and also when used terminally; long *s* is used medially, initially, and in *st* ligatures. In abbreviations note *-ur* is indicated by ᵘ.

Text printed in: *The Vision of William concerning Piers Plowman together with Vita de Dowel, Dobet, et Dobest . . . by William Langland*, ed. W. W. Skeat (E.E.T.S., o.s., no. 54, 1873).

Another specimen in: Pal. Soc., ser. ii, pl. 56.

Our plate shows fol. 43ᵛ (text, Passus X, lines 327–51, and Passus XI, lines 1–12).

TRANSCRIPTION

Quodcũꝗ ligaueris sup t'rā erit ligatũ ⁊ in celis .

℄ And so ı bı leue lellı . lord me for beode elles
þat pardoun and penaunce . and preıeres don saue
Soules þat han ı sẏnned . seuene tímes dedlí

ᶜ℄ ac to trısten vpon trıenales . treulı me þẏnkeþ
Nẏs nout so sıker for þe soule . certes as dowel
ffor whı ı rede ȝow renkes . þat rıche ben on þıs erþe
vp trıst of ȝoure tresour . trıenales to haue
Be ȝe neuere þe boldere . to breke þe ten hestes
and namelıche ȝe maistres . meıres and íuges
þat han þe welþe of þıs world . and wıse men ben ı holde
To purchassche ȝow pardoun . and þe popes bulles

ᶜ℄ at þe dredfuldaı of dom . whan dede men schulle a rısen
and come alle bıfore crıst . acountes to ȝelde
How we ladden oure líjf her . and hıs lawes kepten
and how we dude daı bı daí . þe dom wíle reherce

℄ a poke ful of pardoun þere . ne prouẏncıals letters
þaw he be ı founde in þe fraterníte . of alle þe fẏue ordres
and haue ındulgences dowblefold . but dowel us helpe
ı sette be pardoun nout a pese . ne a pıe hele

ᶜ℄ ffor whı ı consaile alle crıstone . to god to crıȝe mercí
and to marıȝe hıs moder . be oure mene to hím .
þat god ȝeue us grace here . er we gon hennes
Swıche werkes to worche . whıle we ben here
þat after oure deþdaí . dowel reherce
at þe daí of dome . we dude as he us tauȝte .

Explicıt uísıo Willī de petro plouhman .

THıc ıncıpıt uísío eıusdem Willī de dowel .
hus robed ın russet . ı romede a boute
al a somer sesen . forte seke dowel
and afraínede ful ofte . of folc þat ı mette
ȝif enẏ wıht wıste . wher dowel was at ínne
and what mon he mẏȝte be . of manẏ man ı askede
was neuere wıht ın þıs world . þat wısse me coude
where þat he longede . lasse ne more

℄ Tıl hıt bı ful on a fridaí . to freres ı mette
Maistress of menours . men of gret wıt
ı haılede hem hendelí . as ı hadde ı lered
and preıede for charıte . or þeı passede furþere
ȝif þeı knewe ení cuntre . or costes a boute

Quodcumq; ligaueris sup t̃ā er̃it ligatū ⁊ ĩ cœlis'

¶ Ans so·i bi leue lelli·lord me for beode elles
ꝑat pardoun ans penaunce·ans preieres don saue
soules ꝑat han i synned·seuene times dedli҃ ....
¶ Ac to tristen upon trienales·treuli me ꝑynkeꝥ
nys nout so siker for ꝑe soule·certes as dowel
ffor whi i rede ȝow ꝑenkes·ꝑat riche ben on ꝑis erꝥe
up trist of ȝoure tresour·trienales to haue
be ȝe neuere ꝑe boldere·to breke ꝑe ten hestes
ans nameliche ȝe maistres·meires ans iugges
ꝑat han ꝑe welꝑe of ꝑis world·ans wise men ben i holde
To purchasche ȝow pardoun· ans ꝑe popes bulles ....
¶ At ꝑe dredful dai of dom·whan dede men schulle a risen
ans come alle bifore crist·acountes to ȝelde
how ꝥow lad den oure lyf her·ans his lawes kepten
ans how ꝥow dude dai bi dai·ꝑe dom wile reherce ....
¶ A poke ful of pardoun ꝑere·ne prouincials lettres
ꝑau he be i founde m ꝑe fraternite·of alle ꝑe fyue ordres
ans haue indulgences dowblefolds·but dowel us helpe
q sette be pardoun noȝt a pese·ne a pie hele ....
¶ fforꝥi whi i consaile alle cristene·to gos to crye merci
ans to marie his moder·be oure mene to hĩm.
ꝑat gos ȝeue us grace here·er we gon hennes
Swiche werkes to worche·while we ben here
ꝑat after oure deisdai·dowel reherce
at ꝑe dai of dome·we dude as he us tauȝte ....
¶ Explicit uisio Willm̃ de petro plouhman·

Hic incipit uisio eiusdem Willm̃ de Dowel·
¶ Thus yrobed m russet·i romede a boute
al a somer sesen·forte seke dowel
ans afrainede ful ofte·of folk ꝑat i mette
ȝif eny wiȝt wiste·whey dowel was at inne
ans what mon he myȝte be·of many man i askede
was neuere wiȝt m ꝑis world·ꝑat wisse me conde
wheye ꝑat he longede·lasse ne more ....
¶ Til hyt bi full on a fridai·to freres i mette
maistres of menours·men of gret witt
⁊ hailede hem hendeli·as i hadde i lered
ans preiede for charite·or ꝑei passede furꝑere
ȝif ꝑei knewe eni cuntre·or costes a boute

& kryste hy in siþ done

Bi a mounte on þe morne meryly he rydes
Into a forest ful dep þat ferly watz wylde
Hiȝe hillez on vche a halue & holtwodez vnder
Of hore okez ful hoge a hundreth togeder
Þe hasel & þe haȝþorne were harled al samen
Wiþ roȝe raged mosse rayled aywhere
Wiþ mony bryddez vnblyþe vpon bare twyges
Þat pitosly þer piped for pyne of þe colde
Þe gome vpon Gryngolet glydez hem vnder
Þurȝ mony misy & myre mon al hym one
Carande for his costes lest he ne keuer schulde
To se þe seruy of þat syre þat on þat self nyȝt
Of a burde watz borne oure baret to quelle
& þerfore sykyng he sayde I beseche þe lorde
& Mary þat is myldest moder so dere
Of sum herber þer heȝly I myȝt here masse
Ande þy matynez to-morne mekely I ask
& þerto prestly I pray my pater & aue   & crede
    He rode in his prayere
    & cryed for his mysdede
    He sayned hym in syþes sere
    & sayde Cros Kryst me spede
Nade he sayned hymself segge bot þrye
Er he watz war in þe wod of a won in a mote
Abof a launde on a lawe loken vnder boȝez
Of mony borelych bole aboute bi þe diches
A castel þe comlokest þat euer knyȝt aȝte
Pyched on a prayere a park al aboute
Wiþ a pyked palays pyned ful þik
Þat vmbeteȝe mony tre mo þen two myle
Þat holde on þat on syde þe haþel auysed
As hit schemered & schon þurȝ þe schyre okez
Þenne hatz he hendly of his helme & heȝly he þonkez
Jesus & sayn Gilyan þat gentyle ar boþe

15. London, British Museum, Cotton MS. Nero A. x

'SIR GAWAIN AND THE GREEN KNIGHT' (at fols. 37ʳ–126ʳ) and other alliterative poems composed probably in the last quarter of the fourteenth century.

Written not later than A.D. 1400.

Vellum: 17·3 × 12·3 cm.

Written in one hand of a very individualistic small, sharp, angular character. (The MS. is exceptional among pre-1400 vernacular MSS. in that it has illustrations—to the 'Pearl' at fols. 37, 38, and 'Sir Gawain' at fols. 125ʳ, 125ᵛ, 126ʳ).

Note. 3 is used for *y*-sound, for *gh*, for *w*-sound (e.g. bo3e), and is utilized also for final *s* (see Intro., § 2 and for references, p. xv, n. 2); the most noticeable characteristic of the hand is the use of *t* (t͵) for *tz* or *s*,

'derived evidently from an Anglo-French scribal mannerism' (so Gollancz, intro. to facs., p. 8, and cf. *O.E.D.* on *z*); usual 2-form of *r* after *o*; in *t* the vertical is just above the cross-bar; observe fusion in *de* (ðe) and *þe*; curious form of *w* (ʒ)ʒ)) and ligature for *sch* (chŋ); þ always has 'wyn' form.

Abbreviations offer no difficulty. ꝙ makes its appearance for *quoth*.

Text printed in: *Sir Gawain and the Green Knight*, ed. J. R. R. Tolkien and E. V. Gordon (Oxford, 1925), and I. Gollancz, M. Day, and M. S. Serjeantson (E.E.T.S., O.S., no. 210, 1940).

Facsimile of whole MS. ed. I. Gollancz, *Pearl, Cleanness, Patience and Sir Gawain reproduced from MS. Cotton Nero A. x* (E.E.T.S., O.S., no. 162, 1923).

Our plate shows fol. 105ʳ (text, lines 739–74).

TRANSCRIPTION

⁊ wysse hȳ tu sū wone
Bı á moūte on þe morne meryly he rydes
ınto a forest fuldep þat ferly wat3 wylde
hı3e hılle3 on vche ahalue ⁊ holt wode3 vnder
of hore oke3 ful hoge a hundreth to geder
þe hasel ⁊ þe ha3 þorne were harled al samen
wᵗ ro3e raged mosse rayled aywhere
wᵗ mony brydde3 vnblyþe vpon bare twyges
þat pıtosly þer pıped for pyne of þe colde
þe gome vpon gryngolet glyde3 hem vnder
þur3 mony mísy ⁊ myre mō al hȳ one
carande for hıs custes lest he ne keu' schulde
to se þe seruy of þat syre þat on þat self ny3t
of a burde wat3 borne oure baret to quelle
⁊ þerfore sykȳg he sayde ɪ be seche þe lorde
⁊ mary þat ıs myldest moder so dere
of sū herber þer he3ly ɪ my3t here masse
ande þy matyne3 to morne mekely ɪ ask
⁊ þer to prestly ɪ pray my pat' ⁊ aue   íí ⁊ crede
he rode ī hıs prayere
⁊ cryed for hıs mysdede
he sayned hȳ ī syþes sere
⁊ sayde cros kryst me spede

Nade he sayned hȳ self segge bot þrye
er he wat3 war ī þe wod of a won ī a mote
abof alaūde on alawe loken under bo3e3
of mony borelych bole aboute bı þe dıches
a castel þe comlokest þat euʹ kny3t a3te
pyched on a prayere a park al aboute
wᵗ apyked palays pyned ful þık
þat vmbe te3e mony tre mo þē two myle
þat holde on þat on syde þe haþel auysed
as hıt schemered ⁊ schon þur3 þe schyre oke3
þēne hat3 he hendly of hıs helme ⁊ he3ly he þonke3
ɪesus ⁊ say gılyan þat gentyle ar boþe

15

16. London, British Museum, Additional MS. 32578

'THE PRICKE OF CONSCIENCE' (at fols. 1–103), formerly erroneously attributed to Richard Rolle of Hampole, the Yorkshire hermit and mystic.

Written A.D. 1405 by John Farnelay (see colophon fol. 103ʳ, and cf. Intro., p. xiv) 'capellani manent*is* in bolton' (*added in different ink but contemporary hand*).

Paper: 21 × 14 cm.
Written in cursive not book-hand.
Note. 3 is used for *y*-sound, *gh*-sound, &c. (thus *3it*, *no3t*, &c.); þ always written like a *y* (*y̶*); *y* itself is not normally dotted; *i* has a slanting stroke where necessary to avoid ambiguity; uncial form is always used for *d* (ð); *a* is completely closed; wyn is never used, always *w*, and for *s* the Greek form (σ) is always employed initially and finally (the long *s* only medially)[1]; 2-form of *r* continues still only after *o*.

Abbreviations are normal (' for *er*, ll for *lle*, ᴐ for *ur*, &c.).

Latin quotations are rubricated and capitals at the beginning of each line have red fillings; also in red are the connecting lines or brackets.

Text printed in: *The Pricke of Conscience*, ed. R. Morris (Berlin, 1863).

Another specimen in: New Pal. Soc., ser. ii, pl. 109. Our plate shows fol. 76ʳ (text, lines 6766–812).

TRANSCRIPTION

Als a childe ín his modr' lappe
Dos when he soukes hir' pappe
þ'e fore .j. fynde wryten ín holy wrít
Als Job sais þat witnes hít
Capita aspidū suggent ꝫc'
He sais þai sall sowke for thrist
þe heuedes of neddres on þaī fest
Stronge payne of thrist þen haue þai
When þai sall souke siche venym̄ ay
And for þai walde neu'e blithely
Giffe pore men drynk þᵗ were thristy
To slokyn þair' thrist ne on þaī thynk
Ne noþ'e gif þaī mete ne drynke
Ne of þaī seluē drynke walde spare
No day or þai dronken ware
ffor þı it is right þat þai fele
Brēnand thrist þat neu'e sall kele
þat sall þai haue when þai com̄ þidr'
And sharpe hongr' bothe to gidr'
þat neu'e sall sese als .j. said ore
ffor þes two paynes ar' endeles þore
Of þis saynt Jerome beres witnes
And sais þus als here wryten es
In ī̄f'no erūt fames ꝫ sitis ī̄fíníte
In helle sall be þ'e neu'e is right rist
Endles hongoᴐ ꝫ endles thrist
þe **sexte** payne is gret m'kenes
þat ín helle sall be ay endles
þat is so thikke þat mē may it grape
ffro siche þe synfull sall no3t skape
No h̄te may thynke ne tonge may telle
þe gret m'kenes þat is in helle
Of þe whilke Job shewes vs wele
And sais þe synfull sall grope ꝫ fele
Als mykill m'kenes at mydday
As mydnẏght þat sall last ay
Palpabūt tenebras merídíe sicut media nocte ꝫc'.
In helle sall neu'e be day bot nẏght
þe' brȳnes ay fire bot it giffes no light
Bot 3it þe synfull sal ay se
All þe sorowe þat þ'e sall be

[1] In 'tenebras' (l. 5 from foot) and elsewhere in the MS. Farnelay employs *finally* the B-form of *s* (cf. Capgrave's practice, pl. 21).

Als a childe in his moders lappe
Dos when he soukes hir pappe
Vs for I fynde wryten in holy writ
Als Job sais þat witnes his
Capica appillū suggent &
He sais þan sall sowke for thyst
Vs honesder of meddlos on þat fest
Strange payns of thyst þou haue þan
When þai sall souke ailles venym ay
And for þai skald neuer blithe ly
Gif þeo poro men dryuk yt were thysty
To slokyn þair thyst no on þat thynk
We nold gif þair mete no dryuke
No of þair flesh dyyuke walde spare
No day or þan dronken ware
ffor yf it is put þat yu fole
Brennand thyst þat neuer sall kele
þat sall þai haue when þai coud pyde
And ossirpo hongid bothe to gide
þat neuer sall sese als I said vro
for þeo þeo paynes þe endeles vro
Of þis saynt Jerome beres witnes
And sais yus als here wryten es
Ju ihū eyut famus & eyus fruito
In helle sall be þe neuer is put
Endles hongo & endles thyst
þe sixte payns is gret inkones
þat in helle sall be ay endles
þat is so thikke þat mo may it grape
ffis siche þe synfull sall nozt skape
No lite may thynke ne tonge may tell
þe gret inkones þat is in helle
If þo whilke Job shelwo vs kolo
And sais þe synfull sall grepe & fole
Als myhitt nikones at myday
As mydnyght þat sall last ay
Palpabut tenebras meridie sicut media nocte &c.
Ju helle sall noue be day bot nyght
Vs brynnes ay fire bot it giffes no light
Bot zit þe synfull sall ay se
Kit þe torouble þat þe sall be

go & speche: for als moche as þei spoken in hoz þiotes. And
þeo in Englond haue in ou7 langage & speche. iij. lettres mo
þan þei haue. in hyr. a . b . c . & þis. þ . &. ȝ. þe Whiche be clept
þorn. & ȝogh. Of the londs of Albanye. And of libye. of the
Wellynges for Waschinge of the ephauk. & of sloes schippe.

Nolb sith I haue told ȝou beforn of the holy lond. & of þ contree abouten. & of many Weyes for to go to þ lond. & to þ
mount Synay. & of Babyloyne the more & the lesse. & to oþ place
þ I haue spoken beforn: nolb is tyme ȝif it lyke ȝou for to tell
ȝou of the marches. & Iles. & dyuse beste. & of dyuse folk beȝond
those marches. ffor in þo contrees beȝonden. be many dyuse
contrees. & many grete kyngdomes. þ be departed be the. iiij. flo-
des þ come fro paradys terest'. ffor Mesopotayme & the kyngdom
of Caldee. & Arabye. be betbene the. ij. Ryues of Tygre. & of
Eufrates. And the kyngdom of Mede. & of Psye. be betbene
the ryues of Nile. & of Tygres. And the kyngdom of Syreye
Whereof I haue spoken beforn. & Palestyne & Phenyce: be
betbene Eufrates & the see Medyterrane. The Whiche see
Strecheth in lengthe fro Marrok vpon the see of Spayne: vnto
the grete see so þ it lasteth beȝonde Costantynople. Mij. Mij. Mij.
& xl myles of lombardye. And tolbard the see Octyan in Inde
is the kyngdom of Chithie. þ is all closed wt hilles. And aft
ond Schithie & fro the see of Caspie vnto the flom of Cha-
ny. is Amaȝoyne. þ is the lond of ffemynye. Where þ noman
is but only all Women. And aft is Albanye a full grt reme.
And it is clept Albanye. be cause þ the folk be Whiter þan pau
in oþ marches þo abouten. And in þ contree be so grot hounds
& so stronge. þ þei assaylen hym & sleon ho. And þare aft

17. London, British Museum, Cotton MS. Titus C. xvi

'TRAVELS OF SIR JOHN MANDEVILLE', composed originally in French probably about A.D. 1356.

Written about A.D. 1410–20.

Vellum: 21·3 × 14·7 cm.

The handwriting is similar in date and style but different in visual impression to that in Brit. Mus. Egerton MS. 1982 (another version of Mandeville in a more northern dialect), the hand of which shows some later development (e.g. the 2-form of *r* is used *throughout*). Of the Titus hand Warner writes 'a neat, well-formed hand, varying somewhat in parts . . ., but not enough to make it certain that more than one scribe was employed' (*The Buke of John Maundeuill*, Roxburghe Club, 1889, p. xii).

Note. ʒ used for *y*-sound, *gh*, and *z* (e.g. *Amaʒoyne*, l. 5 from foot: cf. its use for final *s* in Nero A. x, pl. 15). The passage in Mandeville here reproduced is important as giving us the n̄ame of ʒ as 'ʒogh' (in the corresponding passage in Egerton MS. 1982, fol. 60ʳ, the name is given as 'ʒok'). The 2-form of *r* is used after *o* and þ is written in 'wyn'-form (ꝥ); *i* has accent where necessary to avoid ambiguity; note lack of distinction between *n* and *u* (e.g. 'houndes', line 2 from foot). In *t* the vertical is now well above the cross-bar.

Abbreviations: ꝫ at the end of a word is for *es* (in the 'Ludus Coventriae', no. 23, it will do duty for -*ys*), ꝰ is for *er* or *ur*; and ꝑ is for *par* or *per*; ' is used for *e* or *er* and ꝇ for *lle*. The Tironian nota for *and* is now ⁊̄.

Text printed in: *Mandeville's Travels*, ed. P. Hamelius (E.E.T.S., o.s., nos. 153, 154, 1919, 1923).

Our plate shows fol. 60ᵛ.

TRANSCRIPTION

ge ⁊̄ speche ⫶ for als moche as þei speken ín her' throtes . ⦅ And wee ín Englond haue ín our' langage ⁊̄ speche ·ij· lettres mo þan þei haue . ín hir' .a.b.c. ⁊̄ þᵗ ís .þ. ⁊̄ .ʒ. the whiche be clept **þorn ⁊̄ ʒogh. Of the londꝫ of Albanye . and of libye . of the wisshínges for wacchínge of the sphauk . ⁊̄ of Noes schippe.** Now sith ɟ haue told ʒou beforn of the holy lond . ⁊̄ of þᵗ conꞇtree abouten . ⁊̄ of many weyes for to go to þᵗ lond . ⁊̄ to þᵉ mont Synay . ⁊̄ of Babyloyne the more ⁊̄ the less . ⁊̄ to oþ' plaçꝫ þᵗ ɟ haue spoken beforn ⫶ now ís tyme ʒif ít lyke ʒou for to tell ʒou of the marches . ⁊̄ ɟles . ⁊̄ dyu'se bestꝫ . ⁊̄ of dyu'se folk beʒond theise marches . ⦅ ffor ín þo contrees beʒonden⫶ bē many dyu'se contrees . ⁊̄ many grete kyngdomes . þᵗ bē depted be the ·iiij· floꞇdes þᵗ come frō padys . t'restr' . ⦅ ffor Mesopotayme ⁊̄ the kyngdom of Caldee . ⁊̄ Arabye ⫶ bē betwene the .ij. Ryu'es of Tygr' . ⁊̄ of Eufrates . ⦅ And the kyngdom of Mede . ⁊̄ of Psye⫶ bē betwene the ryu'es of Níle . ⁊̄ of Tygres . ⦅ And the kyngdom of Syrie where of ɟ haue spoken beforn . ⁊̄ Palestyne . ⁊̄ Phenícye ⫶ bē betwene Eufrates ⁊̄ the se Medyterrane . ⦅ The whiche see . dureth ín lengthe fro Mayrok vpon the see of Spayne ⫶ vnto the grete see . so þᵗ ít lasteth beʒonde Costantynople . Mⁱ.Mⁱ.Mⁱ. ⁊̄ xl myles of lombardye . ⦅ And toward the see Occyan . î Inde ⫶ ís the kyngdom of Shithie . þᵗ ís all closed wᵗ hilles . ⦅ And aft' vnd' Schithie . ⁊̄ fro the see of Caspie vnto the flom of Thaꞇmy⫶ ís **Amaʒoyne** . þᵗ ís the lond of **ffemynye** . wher' þᵗ noman ís bū only all wōmen . ⦅ And aft' ís Albanye a full gᵉt reme . And ít ís clept **Albanye** ⫶ be cause þᵗ the folk bē whiter' þᵉ þan ín oþ' mᵃrches þᵉ aboutē ⦅ And ín þᵗ contree bē so gret houndꝫ ⁊̄ so stronge ⫶ þᵗ þei assayllen lyoūs ⁊̄ slen hē . ⦅ And þāne aft'

18. London, British Museum, Harley MS. 2278

LIFE OF ST. EDMUND, by John Lydgate, monk of Bury St. Edmunds and (1421–32) Prior of Hatfield Broad Oak, Essex (d. probably A.D. 1449).

Written in a pointed English hand (sometimes called 'bastard'), A.D. 1433 (the presentation copy prepared for Henry VI's visit to Bury in that year).

Vellum: 25 × 17·5 cm.

Note. Observe the marked angularity (especially *a, d, e,* &c.), long ascenders and descenders, generally formal, regular and ornate character, lack of cursive features (e.g. letters not joined together)—all idiosyncratic of this pointed hand. Both forms of *r* are used, now generally according to a system—2-form of *r* after *o* and other rounded letters (e.g. *p*), continental *r* with all straight letters. A fine hair stroke is used over *i* (in place of dot) where necessary (e.g. in 'mín'). Round *s* is used finally.

Text printed in: *Altenglische Legenden: Neue Folge,* ed. C. Horstmann (Heilbronn, 1881), pp. 376–414; and *Corolla Sancti Eadmundi,* ed. Lord Francis Hervey, 1907, pp. 409–81.

Our plate shows fol. 66ᵛ (text, lines 904–24).

TRANSCRIPTION

WYth wepyng terys | wıth voıs most lamentable
So as they souhte | walkyng her and ther
Where artow lord | our kyng most agreable
Wher artow Edmond | shew vs thyn heuenly cher
The hed answerde thryes | her | her | her
And neuer cesıd | of al that longe day
So for to crye | tyl they kam | where he lay

Thıs heuenly noıse | gan ther hertıs lyhte
And them releue | of al ther heuynesse
Namly whan they hadde | of the hed a syhte
Kept by a wolff | foryetyng hıs woodnesse
Al thıs considered | they meekly gan hem dresse
To thanke our lord | knelyng on the pleyn
ffor the gret myracle | whıch that they haue seyn

They thouhte | ıt was a merueıle ful vnkouth
To heere thıs language | of a dedly hed
But he that gaff ınto the assıs mouth
Swych speech of old | rebukyng ín hıs dreed
Balaam | the prophete | for hıs vngoodlyheed
The same lord | lıst of hıs grete myht
Shewen thıs myracle | at reu'ence of hıs knyht

With wepyng teerys with vois most lamentable
So as they souhte walkyng her and ther
Where artow lord our kyng most agreable
Wher artow Edmond shew vs thyn heuenly cher
The hed answerde thryes her her her
And neuer cesid of al that longe day
So far to crye tyl they cam where he lay

This heuenly noise whan ther hertis hyhte
And them releue of al ther heuynesse
Namly whan they hadde of the hed a syhte
Kept by a wolff foryetyng his woodnesse
Al this considered they meekly than hem dresse
To thanke our lord knelyng on the pleyn
ffor the gret myracle which that they haue seyn

They thouhte it was a meruetle ful vnkouth
To heere this language of a dede hed
But he that gaff into the assis mouth
Which speech of old rebukyng in his dreed
Balaam the prophete for his vngood hheed
The same lord lift of his grete myght
Shewen this myracle at reuerence of his knyht

I n Eustones legende which late was wrote : stilyo hath preysing armyd
O ur muse now more mylde & loffd strynges : i songe shal gyn to telle
W rth whatt maners : and w{t} whatt love : th{o} dred pute rulyd the worlde
W rth whos preyers he hyst be mevyd to clothe hym in hys robys
A nd grantid to yow the stite to tike : as consulers vsid before.

Benyguyte is destryed techyng stilyo the prynce .

T he keper of the worlde elementas tilhd : which chase hir first place
I n iupiters gudil thatt partith a sundir : grete hetis fro {th}{t} colde
W hich grettest is namyd of hevenly duellers : for elemes furst had ruthe
O f the vnshaply begynnyng worlde : wha al prng lackid dien feine
A nd with her bright chere put thirkenes aside : yibyng lizte to erthys
T his goddesse the stilyo as temple vsith : & as offryng itt alwtys
W here frankentens and swete odourys : to hir w{t} fire is yove
H er prinapal sees : high in thy brest : she hath provided to be
T he techyng eour that thou sholdist deme : & nevir as manhode holde
D o man reioise a nothirs peyne : or othirs deth desire
T hatt in thi peas thou sholdist so breke : cruel martyrs decrees
A s by the to louge hatterede : occasion uoon werre yove.
T hat to trespassours thou sholdist pardon : such astid graunte
A nd ire sone shuldist put away : seldome thou shuldist it medle
O unmevable thou owist not endure : wha benygue preyers be offrd
T o truthe distourbe al adversaurt : and thingis to the submytted
N evir sett i herte as the lyon doeth : which   ouerthrow w{t} wilde borhis
A nd smaler beestis lettyth reune beside : not occnys vpon h{m} lokith
T hus by clemens taught is stilyo : as childa enformyd by maistresse .

Elemeas dwel
lith in the mid
de gudil for
sche is not hoot
w{t} veniabus
ne coolde w{t}
pusillanuuite

19. London, British Museum, Additional MS. 11814

CLAUDIAN'S 'DE CONSULATU STILI-CONIS', accompanied by translation into English unrhymed verses (at fols. 4ʳ–25ʳ).

Written A.D. 1445 at Clare, Suffolk (see colophon, fol. 25ʳ), and certainly executed for Richard, Duke of York (the Yorkist badges of fetterlock, falcon, &c., are in initials at the beginnings of the four parts of the poem).

Vellum: 22 × 15 cm.

Written in small spiky English book-hand. (Manly and Rickert (*The Text of the Canterbury Tales*, i, p. 199) describe the handwriting of the Canterbury Tales MS., Harley 1758 (their Ha²), as of 'general stiff, professional type, a degenerate form of the book-hand in B.M. Add. 11814' (i.e. the present MS.).)

Note. ȝ used only for *gh* (*y* for the *y*-sound), otherwise ordinary *g* (looking very much like an 8); *y* is dotted to avoid ambiguity and *i* has a hair-stroke accent for the same reason where necessary; Greek form of *s* (*σ*) is used finally, otherwise long *s*; 2-form of *r* still used only after *o*.

Abbreviations infrequent; Tironian nota for *and* is ⁊.

Text printed in: E. Flügel, 'Eine mittelenglische Claudian-übersetzung', *Anglia*, xxviii (1905), pp. 255–99 (text), 421–38 (discussion).

Another specimen in: Pal. Soc., ser. i, pl. 200.

Our plate shows fol. 6ʳ (text, lines 1–24).

TRANSCRIPTION

The first parte
Preface .

IN Ruffynes legende which late was write ꞏ stilico hath preysing armyd
Our muse now more mylde . wᵗ losyd stryngis ꞏ ī songe shal gyn to telle
With what maners . and wᵗ what love ꞏ this dred pʳince rulyd the worlde
With whos preyers he lyst be mevid to clothe hím ín his roobys
And grauntid oo yere the state to take ꞏ as consulers vsid before .

Benygnyte is descryed techyng stilico the prynce .

The keper of the worlde Clemencia callyd ꞏ which chase hir first place .J.
In ſupiters girdil that partith a sundir ꞏ grete hetis frō p̄ colde
Which grettest is namȳd of hevenly duellers ꞏ for clemēs first had ruthe
Of the vnshaply begȳnnȳng worlde ꞏ whā al þíng lackid dieu forme
And with her bright chere put thirkenes aside ꞏ ywȳng liȝte to erthys
This goddesse the stilico as temple vsith ꞏ ⁊ as offryng at awtrys
Where frankencens and swete odourys ꞏ to hir wᵗ fire is yove
Her príncipal sees . high ín thy brest ꞏ she hath provided to be .
The techyng evir that thou sholdist deme ꞏ ⁊ nevir as manhode holde .
Oo man reioise a nothirs peyne ꞏ or othirs deth desire .
That ín thi peas thou sholdist so breke ꞏ cruel martys decrees
As by the to longe haterede ꞏ occasion noon were yove .
That to trespassours thou sholdist pardon ꞏ frely askid graunte
And Ire soone shuldist put awey ꞏ seldome thou shuldist it meve
Onmevable thou owist not endure ꞏ whā benygne preyers be offrid
To truthe distroye al aduersaunt ꞏ and thíngis to the submytted
Nevir sett ī herte as the lyon dooth ꞏ which [*word erased*] ovirthrowith wilde boolys
And smaler beestis lettyth renne beside ꞏ not oonys vpon hē lokith
Thus by Clemens taught is stilico ꞏ as childe enformyd by mastresse .

Clemēcia dwel lith ín the mid de girdil ꞏ ffor sche ᴵˢ‖ not hoot wᵗ venſawns ne coolde wᵗ pusillanímite

20. London, British Museum, Arundel MS. 327

'LEGENDYS OF HOOLY WUMMEN', by Osbern Bokenham, Austin Friar of Stoke-by-Clare, Suffolk.

Written A.D. 1447 by Friar Thomas Burgh at Cambridge (see colophon fol. 193ʳ) (*but several hands appear to be involved*).

Vellum: 17 × 12·5 cm.

Written in a close-knit straightforward gothic bookhand; not comfortable to read.

Note. w is used throughout; wyn form of þ used, and Greek form of s. Note fusion in *be, do*, &c.

Abbreviations normal.

Text printed in: *Bokenham's Legendys of Hooly Wummen*, ed. M. S. Serjeantson (E.E.T.S., o.s., no. 206, 1938).

Another specimen in: Pal. Soc., ser. ii, pl. 58.

Our plate shows fol. 91ᵛ (text, lines 4982–5009).

TRANSCRIPTION

The plocutorye into Marye Mawdel' lyf

The yer of gᵃce pleynly to descryue
A thowsand fourhūdryd fourty ⁊ fyue
Aftyr þe cherche of Romys cōputacyoun
Wych wyth Jane chaungyth hyr calculacyoū
Whan Phebus wych nowher ıs mansonarye
Stedefastly but ych day doth varye
Hys herberwe among þe syngnys twelue
As þe fyrste meuer ordeynyd hym selue
Descendyd was ın hys cours adoun
To þe lowest part by cyrcūuolucyoun
Of þe Zodyac cercle Ҫaprycorn ɉ mene
Wher of heythe degrees he hath but fyftene
And n̩d hys retur had sūwhat bygūne
By wych oo degre oonly he had wūne
In clymbyng . ⁊ drow towerd Agnarye
But ın þıs matʼ what shuld ɉ lenger tarye
I mene pleynly up on þat festful eue
In wych as alle crystene men byleue
Thre kyngys her dylygence dede applye
Wyth thre yıftys newe born to gloryfye
Cryst aftyr hys byrthe þe threttende day
Comyng frō þe est ın ful royal aray
By conduct of a sterre wych shone clerʼ
In pʼsence ɉ was of þe lady bowserʼ
Wych ıs also clepyd þe coūtesse of hu
Doun conueyıd by þe same pedegru
That þe Duk of york ıs come for she
Hys sustyr ıs ın egal degre

The yer of gce pleynly to descryue
A thowsand fourhudryd fourty & fyue

.1445.

Aftyr ye cherche of Romys computacyoun
Wych wyth Iane chaungyth hyr calculacyou
Whan phebus wych nowher is mansouarye
Stedefastly but ych day doth uarye
hys herberwe amoung ye syngnys twelue
As ye fyrste meuer ordynyd hym selue
Descendyd was in hys cours adwun
So ye lowest part by cyrcinolucyoun
Of ye zodyaq cercle Capricorn I mene
Wher of heyþe degrees he hath but fyftene
Andns hys retur had sumwhat bygune
By wych oo degre only he had wune
In clymbyng & drow toward Aquarye
But in þis mat what shuld I lenger tarye
I mene pleynly up on yat festful eue
In wych as alle crystene men byleue
Thre kyngys her dylygence dede applye
Wyth thre giftys newe born to glorysye
Cryst aftyr hys byrthe ye threttende day
Comyug fro ye est in ful royal aray
By conduct of a sterre wych shone clee

domina Botoser
comitissa &c

In psence I was of ye lady buwce
Wych is also cleppd ye countesse of hu
Doun conueyed by ye same pedygru

Dux Eborum

That ye duk of york is come for she
hys sustyr is in egal degre

To my wel beloued in our lord god ꝺ̄ nicholas
maystir of ye ordre of sympryngha
Whech ordre is entytled on to ye
name of seynt gilbert / ffreir J C.
a mong doctouris left sende re-
uerens as to swech dignyte desiryng clennesse
to 3our soule and helth to 3our body Now
with mine felbe dyyes bat3 notyfied on
to me bat ye lyf of our fader seynt augus-
tyn Whech bat J trauslat in to our tunge
at instaunce of a certeyn Thoma was broht
to 3our presens Whech lykyd 3ou wel as it
is told saue 3e Wold J schul adde 3to alle
3oo relygyous bat lyue vndyr his reule
but to 3is J ansewerd bat it was not my thur-
the but if men like for to knowe ye mater
diffusely yei may lerne it in a sermon bat seid
at cambryg ye 3er be fore myn opposicion
Whech sermon vmbshap J Wil sette in englisch
in ye last ende of ye werk Than aftir 3e
had red ye lyf of seynt augustin 3e payde
to on of my frendes bat 3e desired gretly
ye lyf of seynt gilbert schuld be trauslat
in the same forme Thus mad he instaunce
to me and J grauuted both 3our petycion for / tha
J schuld not frustrate him of his meditacion
To ye honour of god and of all seyntis 3u
Wil we begynne yis tretys namelych for the
solitaryo ꝺ̄me of 3our relygion Whech vn

21. London, British Museum, Additional MS. 36704

LIVES OF ST. AUGUSTINE OF HIPPO AND ST. GILBERT OF SEMPRINGHAM, &c., by John Capgrave, Austin Friar of King's Lynn, Norfolk (d. 1464), author also of the 'Liber de Illustribus Henricis' and a Chronicle of England (to 1417).

Written A.D. 1451 (the year of the composition of the Life of St. Gilbert, cf. fol. 116ʳ) probably by Capgrave himself (the hand agreeing with that in Cambridge University Library MS. Gg. 4. 12). (On the question of Capgrave's *autograph* MSS. see H. M. Bannister in *Ye Solace of Pilgrimes: A Description of Rome, circa A.D. 1450 by John Capgrave*, ed. C. A. Mills (Oxford, 1911), pp. xv–xxii.)

Paper: 20·5 × 14·3 cm.

Handwriting is neat and regular but individual and not calligraphic; corrections are in same hand as text.

Note. th is used in place of þ for capitals and at the end (and sometimes the beginning) of words; þ itself appears in the degenerate 'wyn' form; the 2-form of r is not used; ʒ is used for only y-sound (e.g. 'ʒour'); g itself is written like y with a cross-bar added (ꝗ); long s except finally, when round s is used (the latter characteristically in Capgrave's hand rather like a small-size в; cf. also pl. 16); y is sometimes dotted.

Abbreviations: it is a question whether the ' after r is for 're' or whether it has become now a meaningless scribal flourish, nor is it certain whether the '-es' symbol (ę) after g in 'among' (l. 5) is to be extended or not. Again, in words such as 'petycioun' (e.g.) it is doubtful whether the scribe had in mind oū or oñ when he wrote the last two letters.

Text printed in: *John Capgrave's Lives of St. Augustine and St. Gilbert of Sempringham*, ed. J. J. Munro (E.E.T.S., o.s., no. 140, 1910).

Also reproduced with another page in: New Pal. Soc., ser. i, pl. 70.

Our plate shows fol. 46ʳ.

TRANSCRIPTION

TO my wel beloued ın our' lord god
maystır of þe order' of sįmpỹghām
whech ordre ıs entytled on to þe
name of seynt gılbert ȷ ffrer' J.C.
a mongę doctourıs lest sende re⸍
uerens as to swech dıgnyte desırīg clēnesse
to ʒour' soule and helth to ʒour' body Now
with ınne fewe dayes was notyfıed on
to me þat þe lyf of our' fader seynt augus⸍
tỹn whech þat ȷ transạlat ın to our' tūge
at ınstaūs of a c'teyn womā was browt
to ʒour' presens whech lykyd ʒow wel as ıt
ıs told saue ʒe wold ȷ schul adde þ'to alle
þoo relygyous þat lyue vndyr hıs reule
But to þıs ȷ answer' þat ıt was not my char⸍
ge but ıf men lıke for to knowe þıs mater'
dıffusely þeı may lerne ıt ın a s'mō þatˬseıd
at cambrıg' þe ʒer' befor' myn opposıcıoū
whech s'mon vnphap ȷ wıl sette ın englısch
ın þe last ende of þıs werk Than aftır ʒe
had red þıs lyf of seynt augustỹ ʒe sayde
to on of my frendes þat ʒe desıred gretly
þe lyf of seynt gılbert schuld be translat
ın the same forme Thus mad he ınstaūce
to me and ȷ graūted both ʒour' petycıoū ˳ for ˳ ꝫ hıs
ȷ wold not frustrate hım of hıs medıacıoū
To þe honour' of god and of al seyntıs þā
wıl we begỹne þıs tretys namelych for the
solıtarye womē of ʒour' relıgıoū whech vn⸍

M. Nıcholas
Reysby

22. Oxford, Bodleian Library, Rawlinson MS. B. 408

REGISTER OF CHARTERS, &c., of the Benedictine nunnery of Godstow, near Oxford, paraphrased in English, with explanatory prologue, for the use of the nuns in the time of Dame Alice Henley (elected Abbess A.D. 1445–51; d. A.D. 1470).

Written probably between A.D. 1450 and A.D. 1460 (with additions made as late as A.D. 1473).

Vellum: 33 × 22·3 cm.

Written in an English book-hand of a type common about the middle of the fifteenth century.

Note. *y* is habitually dotted, the scribe is erratic in the use of a diacritic mark for *i*; *th* is usually written out but þ also occurs occasionally (written in 'wyn' form), and *s* is followed by a fine nearly vertical stroke.

Abbreviations: *ll* have a horizontal stroke (e.g. 'all') and final *r* is frequently followed by ' (e.g. 'wer ' '); the purpose being in each case presumably but not certainly to indicate the presence of final *e* (it may however have become merely a scribal mannerism).

Text printed in: *The English Register of Godstow Nunnery, near Oxford*, ed. A. Clark (E.E.T.S., o.s., nos. 129, 130, 142, 1905–11).

Also reproduced in: New Pal. Soc., ser. i, pl. 196.

Our plate shows fol. 13ʳ (upper half only).

TRANSCRIPTION

The prolog' of the englẏssh regist'.   ·I·

T he wẏseman tawht hẏs chẏld gladlẏ to rede bokẏs and hem well vndur
stonde . for ın defaute of vndẏrstondẏng ıs oft tẏmes causẏd neclẏgence
hurte harme and hẏnderaunce as expẏence prevẏth ın manẏ a place . and
for asmuche as women of relẏgẏone ⁱⁿ redẏnge bokẏs of latẏn bẏn excusẏd of grete vndur=
stondẏng where ıt ıs not her modẏr tonge . Therfore how be hẏt that theẏ wolde rede
her' bokẏs of remembraunce and of her' munẏmentẏs wrẏte ın latẏn for defaute of undur=
stondẏng theẏ toke ofte tẏmes grete hurt and hẏndraunce and what for defaute of trewe
lernẏd men that all tẏmes be not redẏ hem to teche and counsaẏl . and feere also ⁊ drede
to shewe her' euẏdence opẏnlẏ that oftẏntẏme hath causẏd repentaunce . Hẏt wer' ryht ne=
cessarẏ as hẏt semẏth to the undẏrstondẏng of suche relẏgẏus women that theẏ mẏht haue
out of her latẏn bokẏs sum wrẏtẏnge ın her' modẏr tonge wherebẏ theẏ mẏht haue bettẏr
knowlyge of her' munẏmentẏs and more clereˡʸ yeue ınformacẏon to her seruauntẏs rent
gedurarẏs and receẏuowrs ın the absent of her' lernẏd councell . Wher'fore a pore brodᵒ
and welwyller'   to the goode Abbas of Godstowe Dame
Alıce henleẏ and to all hẏr couent the whẏch bẏn for the more ptẏ ın englẏssh bokẏs
well ẏ lernẏd hertẏlẏ desyrẏng the worshẏp profẏt and welfare of that deuoute place
that for lak of vndurstondẏng her' munẏntẏs [*sic*] sholde ın no damage of her' lẏflod her'
aftur fallẏn . In the worshẏp of our' ladẏ and seẏnt Iohn Baptıst patron of thẏs
seẏd monasterẏ the sentence for the more ptẏe of her munẏmentẏs conteẏnẏd ın the
boke of her regẏstr' ın latẏn aftẏr the same forme and ordẏr of the seẏd boke hath pur=
posẏd wᵗ goddẏs grace to make aftur hẏs conceẏt fro latẏn ınto englẏssh sētencẏoslẏ
as foloweth thẏs sẏmple translacıon ·;· The cronıcle of the hows and Monas=
terı of Godstoᵂ makẏth mensẏon how that place wace fowndẏde fẏrst bẏ
reuelacẏon ın thẏs wẏse ın wẏnchestre

The prologe of the hole englisshe reule

...

Hic incipit de suscitacione lazari.

Lord þat all thyngis dede make of noght
And puttyst oþer qualitys to þe' sernannce
Haue they handworke & þ' hast wroght
As þu art lord of þyz substannce
O gracyous god at þi plesannce
of my dysese nolt comforte me
Which goddis syknes hath such penauúnce
an oþyr ffor good kepe may i nolt se

Systyr martha & magdelyn eke
þt hast helpe me in bedde to dresse
ffor treuly I am so woundydly seke
I may nolt skepe ye gyett sekues
my doth to cowm nolt I gesse
helpe into chambur þt I be led
my grett dysesse I haue yat losse
If I wer leyd upon a bed

Lazarus brother be of good cher
I hope ye syknes tygyt wol yat skake
vpon yr bed yst zow wyth her
And a good slep assay to take

Pese gentyl brothyr ffor goddys sake
lyfte up zour herte & be not faynt
an hevy houssholde it vs ze make
If dedly syknes haue zow atoynt

ffor sothe der systoyn I may not skepe
my syknes so sar doth dyr encrece
of me I pray zow take wyth good kepe
tyll þt my payne be gynne to cese

23. London, British Museum, Cotton MS. Vespasian D. viii

'LUDUS COVENTRIAE': the compiler's book of a collection of mystery plays, preceded (fols. 1ʳ–9ᵛ) by a 'Proclamation' which was composed in its present form in close connexion with the compilation of the series and describes the 'pageants' to be acted. The title (quite erroneous) is due to Sir Robert Cotton's librarian, Richard James (d. A.D. 1638).

Written between A.D. 1450 and A.D. 1475 mostly by one scribe.

Paper: 20·3 × 14 cm.

The writing is characteristic of the period; variations in it are probably due to different parts being written at different times.

Note. ᴣ is still used for *y*-sound and the *gh*-sound, and utilized for *z* (as in 'Lazarus'); Greek *s* (σ) is used for final *s*; χ for *x* (i.e. *sh* in 'he χall be') is carefully distinguished by the scribe from ꝑ for *pro* (e.g. 'ꝑfesse'); the 2-form of *r* after *o* and *y* (e.g. 'brothyᴣ'). The tag to the *n* appears to have no significance and *tt* in, for example, 'all' *may* or may not be for *lle*.

Abbreviations are frequent; ꝭ at the end of words is in this MS. to be expanded as *ys*; the mark ' is used for *n* and *m* and elsewhere, while ꝯ for *con* is used once (on fol. 112ʳ).

Text in: *Ludus Coventriæ or The Plaie called Corpus Christi: Cotton MS. Vespasian D. viii*, ed. K. S. Block (E.E.T.S., E.S., no. cxx, 1922).

Another specimen in: New Pal. Soc., ser. ii, pl. 92.

Our plate shows fol. 127ᵛ.

TRANSCRIPTION

híc íncípít de suscítacõe lazarí .

❡ Lazarus

Ｇod þᵗ all thynge dede make of nowth
And puttyst eche creatur' to hís fenaunce
Saue thyn handwerke þᵗ þᵘ hast wrought
As þᵘ art lord of hyᴣ substauns
O gracyous god at þⁱ plesaûs
of my dysese now comforte me
which þᵅowe syknes hath such penawnce
on ethys ffor heed Ache may j now se

❡ Systyr Martha ⁊ Mawdelyn eke
Wᵗ hast helpe me ín bedde to dresse
ffor trewly j am so woundyrly seke
j may nevyr schape þis grett seknes
my deth ís com now j gesse
help ínto chawmer' þᵗ j be led
my grett desesse j hope χal lesse
If j wer' leyd upon a bed

———————————————————Martha

❡ lazarus brother be of good cher
I hope ᴣ0ᵅ syknes Ryght wel χal slake
vpon þis bed rest ᴣow rygh[t] her
And a good slep assay to take

———————————————————Magdalyn

Now jentyl brothyr ffor goddys sake
lyfte up ᴣowr' herte ⁊ be not feynt
An hevy housholde wᵗ vs ᴣe make
If dedly syknes haue ᴣow Ateynt

———————————————————lazarus

❡ ffor sothe der' systeryn j may not slepe
my syknes so sor' doth evyr encrese
of me j pray ᴣow take ryght good kepe
tyll þᵗ my peyne be gynne relese

———————————————————Martha

23

24. London, British Museum, Lansdowne MS. 285

'SECREES OF OLD PHILISOFFRES', by John Lydgate and Benedict Burgh, an English version of the pseudo-Aristotelian 'Secreta Secretorum' (at fols. 152ʳ–196ᵛ).

Written before A.D. 1469 by William Ebesham for Sir John Paston (included in a bill submitted by Ebesham probably in A.D. 1469, the original of which is now Brit. Mus. Additional MS. 43491, fols. 12, 13). On Ebesham's handwriting see A. I. Doyle, 'The Work of a late Fifteenth-Century English Scribe, William Ebesham',

Bulletin of the John Rylands Library, xxxix (1957), pp. 298–325.

Paper: 30 × 21·5 cm.

Note. 2-form of *r* is used not only after *o* but is now normal form with this shape ⁊; tall *a* (ɑ) alternates with ordinary *a*; *g* is written like *y* with a cross-bar (cf. pl. 21); *y* is usually dotted; þ appears like 'wyn' (ƿ); in combinations *th* and *ght* the *h* has a horizontal stroke through ascender; as do *ll* (e.g. in 'all').

Text printed in: *Lydgate's and Burgh's Secrees of Old Philisoffres*, ed. R. Steele (E.E.T.S., E.S., no. lxvi, 1894).

Our plate shows fol. 152ʳ (text, lines 1–28).

TRANSCRIPTION

❬ *This is the book of goverunce .* ❭
of kynges and Prynces .

God almyghty saue and conferme oure kyng .
In all vertu to his encrees of glorie .
His Reame and hym by pollitik lyvyng .
With drede and loue to haue memorie
Of his Enemyes conquest and victorye
With septre and swerde twene both to do right
Aftir' his lawes to eu'y maner wight

❬ ffirst in all vertu to sett his governaunce
The lorde to please and his lawes kepe .
And his lieges with hartly obeisaunce .
In pees to kepe them where they wake or slepe
To punysshe Tirauntę and cherisshe them þᵗ be meke
With two cleere eyen of discretion
As ye them fynde of disposicion .

❬ Them that bee gode cherisshe them in godenesse
and them that be frowarde of Corage
Peise the balaunce by grete avisenesse
ffor loue nor hate doo noon outrage
Set a gode mene betwene olde ⁊ yong of age
Excellent prynce this ꝑcesse to compile
Takith at gree . the Rudenesse of my style

❬ ffirst j that am humble s'uytoure
Of the kyng with hole affection
voide of Eloquence j haue dooñ my laboⁱ
To sett in Order and execucõn
ffirst my seemplesse vndir' correctõn
wᵗ right hole hert in my best entent
for to accomplissh your comaundment

This is the book of governaunce
of kynges and princes

God almyghty save and conferme owre kyng
In all partie to his encrees of glorie
His reame and hym by pollitik lyvyng
With drede and love to have memorie
Of his enemyes conquest and victorie
With septre and sworde theme both to do pusshe
After his lawes to every maner wight

Auyse in all ye that sett his order nammes
The lorde to please and his lawes kepe
And his leges with hertly obeysaunce
In pees to kepe them whate they wake or slepe
To punysshe tyranny and cherisshe them yt be meke
With thos elders even off dyrection
As ye them fynde off dysposicion

Them that be gode cherisshe them in godenesse
And them that be frowarde of corage
Peyse the balaunce by grete avisenesse
For love nor hate do noon outrage
Bot a gode mene betwene olde & yong of age
Excellent prynce this passe to compile
Takith at gree the rudenesse of my style

First I that am humble enjtente
Of the kyng with hole affection
Voide of eloquence I have doon my labo
To sett in order and correccion
First my semplesse vndw correction
To pytt hole hert in my best entent
For to accomplisshe your commaundment